EDUCATION, PARTICIPATION AND EMPOWERMENT

MOTIVATION AND HUMAN DEVELOPMENT SERIES
General Editor : **PRAYAG MEHTA**

No. 1 Social Achievement Motivation: Needs, Values and Work Organization
Prayag Mehta

No. 2 Education, Participation and Empowerment: Studies in Human Development
Prayag Mehta

No. 3 Work, Public Systems and Human Development
Prayag Mehta

About the Author

Prof. Prayag Mehta has worked in various fields closely related to social and human development. He has taught and researched at several universities and institutions. He has to his credit wide-ranging publications including books on issues pertaining to literacy, education, psychology, development, management and labour. He was Director, National Labour Institute, New Delhi, and is currently working with the Participation and Development Centre, New Delhi. He is the General Editor of the Series on Motivation and Human Development.

Motivation and Human Development Series-2

General Editor : **Prayag Mehta**

EDUCATION, PARTICIPATION AND EMPOWERMENT

Studies in Human Development

PRAYAG MEHTA

CONCEPT PUBLISHING COMPANY, NEW DELHI 110059

ISBN 81-7022-569-8

First Published 1995

Published and Printed by
Ashok Kumar Mittal
Concept Publishing Company
A/15-16, Commercial Block, Mohan Garden
NEW DELHI 110059 (India)

To
Social activists of Kotra, Udaipur
District of Rajasthan,
and
Singari, Ranchi District
of Bihar

General Editor's Introduction

We are happy to release this second volume : *Education, Participation and Empowerment : Studies in Human Development* in the Series on *Motivation and Human Development.*

Human development is now emerging as an important movement around the world. The present volume consists of studies of : elementary education, adult education, welfare of unorganized workers, skill formation in women, participation of people in socio-economic development, youth aspirations for education and development and organization and empowerment of the poor. As the worldwide experience suggests, organized interventions on the part of the people and socially conscious public action could make a significant difference in achieving the goals of human development, even under the existing conditions of poverty. It is hoped that the present volume, based on grassroot experience and people's self-action, would make a useful contribution toward promoting human development in the country.

PRAYAG MEHTA

Acknowledgement and Preface

THE present work has evolved over a number of years. Some of the chapters are revised, enlarged and updated versions of my earlier papers as follows:

Chapter 2 has used "Socio-Psychological Interventions for Universalizing Education," *Vikalap*, 1977, Vol. 2 (1), 59-73, and "Education Oriented Development Strategy : Universalization of Elementary and Adult Education" presented at a "National Seminar on New Education Policy", Faculty of Management Studies, University of Delhi, Sept. 27-28, 1985; Chapter 3 : "Young Workers Aspirations and Development," *Youth Affairs*, 1979, 1, 1-14; Chapter 4 : "Welfare of Unorganized Workers : The Case of Central Welfare Organization," *Vikalap*, 1985 10(3), 279-302; Chapter 6 : "Tribal Youth Camps : Education for Participatory Organization of Rural Poor", *NLI Monograph*, 1979, 2/79; "Participatory Education of Rural Workers : People's Self-Action for Social Development," *NLI Bulletin*, 1983, 9(3&4), 199-219; Chapter 8 : "Organizing for Empowering the Poor," *Men and Development*, 1987, 3, 49-59; and Chapter 9 has used "Political Efficacy and Participation in Socio-Economic Development," *Journal of Rural Development*, 1983, 2(6), 563-570; and (with Chandra Navin) *People's Self Development Action : The Case of Singari*, New Delhi : NLI, 1984. Thanks are due to the above journals for permission to use the published material for the present book.

The field-work for various studies was done in Orissa, Bihar, Madhya Pradesh, Uttar Pradesh, West Bengal, Rajasthan, Karnataka and some other places in the country. First and foremost, thanks are due to a large number of people, both men and women, scattered in several districts of the country, who actively participated in various activities in connection with the above studies and contributed many insights and ideas. A number of district-level officials and my erstwhile colleagues at the National Labour Institute actively contributed to the various studies. Their help is gratefully acknowledged.

Thanks are also due to Shri Ashok Mittal and his team at the Concept Publishing Company for their care in processing the volume for publication; and to Shri Jagdish Singh, who provided the necessary secretariat assistance in preparing the various drafts. But for his patience and continuous help, the book would not have taken this final shape.

Special thanks are, however, due to the social activists of Singari, Ranchi District of Bihar, and the Kotra area of Udaipur District of Rajasthan for their active involvement in and initiative for the projects reported here; and to whom, the book is dedicated.

PRAYAG MEHTA

Contents

List of Figures

List of Tables

1

INTRODUCTION

1.1. The Social and Psychological Scenario : Implications for Human Development

ONE of the major failures in India has been the non-fulfilment of the Constitutional directive for universal elementary education. In addition to inadequate enrolment, the school system has been suffering from large-scale dropout, thus, directly contributing to the continuing backlog of illiteracy. A large number of empirical and other studies have been conducted, from time to time, to identify the causes of non-performance in elementary education. Taken together, findings of such research bring out socio-economic factors, such as poverty, nutritional and cultural deprivation as the major causes of this continuing problem. Studies have also brought out the importance of curriculum and text-books, medium of instruction, system of examination, management of education, absence of pre-school education, treachers' motivation and their attitudes as another chunk of important causes of this problem. However, as discussed in Chapter 2, such variables interact among themselves, contributing to the continuing failure of elementary education. Interestingly, despite various committees and commissions and policy prononcements, the entrenched problems have continued unabated.

Capability Building : The Core of Human Development

Education is critical to economic policies and ecological considerations. Not only technical knowledge and capability are built up but new values are created and individuals and societies are enabled to cope with the rapidly changing social, environmental and developmental realities. Literacy is essential for preparing people to break out from their age-old social stranglehold and to act on their environment.

Importance of education and social development is borne out by the National Sample Survey (NSS) data in India. Illiterate families are unable to take advantage of the basic health and family planning services. For example, only 11 per cent children of the illiterate households took the triple antigen vaccine (part of free public service) compared to 50 per cent children belonging to the households where parents had primary education (Minhas, 1991). Thus, social development, particularly awareness, enlarges people's capability to obtain access to and utilize health and other services which enrich quality of their life.

As the first Human Development Report (UNDP, 1990) argued, the real purpose of development should be to enlarge people's choices. Lack of education and awareness restricts the cognitive map of individuals, as reported in Chapter 4. Such deprived persons, for example, rural women, are not above to go beyond traditional thinking and make "marketable" vocational choices. They are also not able to have access to health services, as seen in Chapter 5. They also lack capability of enrolling and retaining their children in schools as seen in Chapter 2. "Enhancing their capabilities," as Anand and Sen (1992 : 107) put it, "to function in these elementary ways is what lies at the core of human development."

1.2. Changing Social and Psychological Scenario

Under the Impact of various social and political forces and processes since independence, people now tend to show significant behavioural changes. These are reflected in youth aspirations; people's articulation of their needs and problems, especially women's; and in increasing dissatisfaction with the political regime, particularly with the day-to-day government functioning.

Symbolizing this, one young person in a remote area of Rajasthan, recalling their destitution, remarked, "Nobody listens to us, neither the Minister, nor the Sarpanch now the Patwari." Tribal and rural women in Bihar and Orissa, as reported in Chapter 4, keenly desire to acquire vocational skills to enable them to generate additional income. They were, however, sceptical about government officials' handling of such training programmes. These illiterate, remotely located and marginalized tribal women would rather like to have some kind of their own organization to manage such activities. Such women in Uttar Pradesh repeatedly characterized the State functioning in their own inimitable idiom. They would say, ***hanya len den ke bina koyi kam neyi hota*** (no entitlement can be obtained here without a bribe) (Mehta, 1992). Such images of the government indicate widespread sense of political normlessness. In turn, this indicates increasing political and social awareness and a concern for better performance in State policies and programmes (Mehta, 1994a).

Thus, somewhat educated rural youth and urban-based trade union leaders have been repeatedly asking for better education, better work, better vocational skill formation as well as better economic performance which could increase their access to water, banking, training and other infrastructural facilities. Such goals indicate an emerging motivation for social achievement which seeks and asks for better quality of life (Mehta, 1994a).

An interesting characteristic of the changing social scenario is that behavioural changes are observed not only in somewhat educated village and urban youth, but also in tribal and other rural women. They tend to articulate, sometimes directly, sometimes indirectly, their needs for income generation, skills and greater purchasing power, as brought out in Chapters 3 and 4. Despite limitations of their thinking, they show some concern for a better quality of life for themselves, particularly for their children.

The Predicament : What to do Now?

In the changing scenario, with rising aspirations, the poor, particularly the youth, face a predicament : Which way to go? What to do? During field interviews and discussions and in imaginative story-writing during training courses, the youth project forward-looking choices, as discussed in Chapter 3. They would, for example, say "I also want to learn some mechanical work...I have to learn motor car repair." They also, however, know the reality. They lack material resources to back their choices and are aware of such worldly blocks. They would, for example, imagine (about themselves) "he is thinking about his school fees and other expenses. Thinking what to do now. All are thinking what to do now?" As they, particularly women, would report (Mehta, 1992), "we do not have water, no schooling for children and no work." And those who had work, like the unorganized *beedi* and mica-mine workers, as reported in Chapter 5, dared not to go to hospital even when they suffered from deadly diseases like T.B., lest they lose their job. Medical facilities, howsoever limited, did exist. They were, however, not able to assert and utilize such services.

Moving between Dependence and Assertion

The changing social environment seems to give at least some indication that the socially and economically disadvantaged youth and women yearn now to assert and to go beyond mere articulation of grievances. They continue to show dependence on influential others and also to crave for subsidies as fantasied by one youth, "We are only thinking this that we should get free facilities from the government." At the same time, as discussed in Chapter 3 and other chapters, they perceive the need for organization saying, "We are five or twenty-five persons. With all united in one organization, only our future work can be completed." While seeking facilities from the government, they also tend to suggest alternatives. For example, as reported in Chapter 4, they want elimination of the interference of the government functionaries in favour of some autonomous institutions for conducting vocational training. There seems to be a shift from dependence to assertion. They show strong attraction for the entrenched subsidy culture. For example, they continue to see the Jawahar Rozgar Yojana (JRY) as another State programme for obtaining some subsidy (Planning Commission, 1992). At the same time, they seem to show increasing attraction for their participation in socio-economic decision-making and in related programmes.

The Talk and Practice of Participation

Although, there has been frequent talk about people's participation, it is hardly actualized. This wide gap between promise and practice, between word and deed, directly contributes to a sense of cynicism and to increasing disillusionment with State functioning. Lack of concern and commitment on the part of the various government implementing agencies is too glaring. For example, as discussed in Chapter 5, statutory welfare programmes for the benefit of unorganized workers suffered from major organizational maladies. There was, on the one hand, lack of focus on objectives in the programme and, on the other, a sense of dissatisfaction and alienation among its own personnel which further reduced the creditability of government organizations and their programme. A sense of resentment seems to pervade throughout the country, in urban as well as rural areas. Such resentment and normlessness seem to go beyond the grievance stage as discussed in Chapters 7 and 8. As reported in Chapter 9 and elsewhere (Mehta, 1994a), grassroot level people's organizations succeed in mobilizing people to participate in self-action projects. Though, participation is emerging as a basic human need (UNDP, 1993), it is not likely to come easily and/or automatically. As participation threatens the established power structure, the bureaucracy may look at it as a law and order problem (Mehta, 1989).

1.3. Organization, Participation and Human Development

People's participation in affairs and processes that affect their lives, thus, seems to emerge as an important human need. The changing social and psychological environment in a developing country like India tends to further accentuate this need. As people participate in socio-economic and political activities, they enhance their capability to do some more effectively, individually and, more particularly, collectively. With an increased sense of competence, people desire to influence and control. This, in turn, brings them in conflict with the vested interests who have been controlling and shaping their destiny for long and who do not want to give up their power. Such conflicts, as discussed in Chapter 8, may further sharpen people's capability for organizing and managing their affairs. Experience, however, shows the need for planned interventions to help them develop the necessary skills and motivation.

Interventions for Facilitating Participation and Organization

It is a measure of the strength of its need and concept that people's participation has been repeatedly recognized as important in government policies and plans. Its need is reiterated for protection of forests and environment, in rural development, in literacy programmes, in fact, in all development programmes.

Besides the inhibitory socio-political forces, the people themselves are not used to participate. There is, therefore, the need for planned interventions such as education, attitudinal change, motivation training, organization building, participatory development efforts, as discussed in Chapters 6, 7 and 8. Such educational and organizational interventions could help mobilize the people, promote solidarity among them and release their energy for participation in meaningful social and economic projects.

Learning from past experience, the Planning Commission had initiated a scheme some time ago for promoting organization of the poor. One such scheme, despite shortcomings, as discussed in Chapter 7, seemed to have generated awareness and helped them to undertake organizing efforts. A review of such a programme showed that mere doling out of information about government programmes hardly helps. Besides well-planned mass campaigns, monitoring, mid-course corrections and educational activities were required, as discussed in Chapter 8, to help them collectively assert for their entitlements. The experience also suggests the need for bureaucratic reorientation and restructuring of administration, capacity building for NGOs and enrichment of content and processes of programmes designed to promote people's organization. Such efforts, as indicated by the functioning of the National Literacy Mission (NLM), require attention to monitoring and managerial resource support for integrating the needs and problems of people with campaigns for education and development (Mehta, 1990; 1992).

The Experience of Interventions

The changing socio-psychological scenario was reflected in active responsiveness and participation of the people in various interventions such as training (Chapter 6), organization and capability building (Chapters 7 and 8) and in development action (Chapter 9). The initial hesitation and apprehension soon gave way to problem-solving approach and collective problem diagnosis. They readily got involved in the various training sessons, thus, facilitating the learning process. They were able to relate their problems to larger socio-economic causes. They showed capability for analyzing and understanding their situation. This helped them to overcome their cynicism and increase awareness about socio- economic problems. Such experience showed that the poor were ready to move from the resentment-and-grievance stage to not only forceful articulation of their needs and problems but to problem-solving and action. The various interventions, therefore, showed a common wavelength.

1.4. Motivation for Social Achievement

Studies, thus, show that education, awareness, organization and participation of people along with enlightened public action/interventions are important for obtaining human development goals. Studies highlight the importance of social achievement motivation which could stimulate high standards of health despite low income. For example, Sri Lanka, China, Chile, Tanzania, etc., and our own State of Kerala have shown human development ahead of their income status. On the other hand, there are countries like Senegal, Guinea, Libya, Saudi Arabia, etc., whose income status has been ahead of their human development. There is, therefore, no automatic link between income and human development (UNDP, 1993 : 15). A concern for others is clearly a crucial ingredient of public action (Dreze and Sen, 1989 : 12-13) which could stimulate human development.

People's movement and collective action not only help people enhance their countervailing power but also help strengthen motivation, as found in the case of field functionaries of a literacy project (Mehta, 1990). Thus, motivation of organizers, leaders and influential others could initiate and organize public action, and help release a process of relearning and empowerment. People are not just consumers and recipients of aid, subsidies and help of the State and other such agencies. Development efforts should seek to empower people to act on the environment and take an actor role in such matters. "The public has to be seen as an agent and not merely as a passive patient" (Dreze and Sen, 1989 : 10). Thus, it is not enough to have projects and programmes like, for example, integrated rural development, primary health services, etc. It is also necessary to facilitate active participation of public in decision-making and management of such programmes. This needs to be done through promotion of skills, education and maintenance of full employment (Dreze and Sen, 1989 : 187; UNDP, 1993 : 21-29).

1.5. Human Development Gains

Education and organization help people achieve some concrete success experience in terms of increased income and self-esteem, as reported in Chapter 9. Experience shows that education, organization and self-action release a process of human development. They are able to raise demand on the system for better performance particularly for education of children, for better health care, and for skill formation to enable them to cope with new challenges. As reported in Chapter 9, not only there was increased enrolment in the elementary classes but also in the literacy classes. People took the initiative in their hands for energizing the entire community for such activities and for obtaining access to various infrastructural facilities including credit, training, economic projects, etc. Education, organization and participation, therefore, seem to lay the foundation for continuing capability and collective action for improving quality of life, with implications for human development.

2

INTERVENTIONS FOR UNIVERSALIZING EDUCATION*

2.1. The Situation in Two Decades—The 1960s and 1970s

THE Indian Constitution provides for compulsory primary education for children in the age group 6-14 years. According to official statistics, (Ministry of Education, 1976) 66.11 million children in the age group 6-11 years, 16.5 million in the age group 11-14 years and 7.9 million in the age group 14-17 years were enrolled in 1974-75. Thus, some 90.5 million children were on the school rolls out of some 154 million (1971 Census) in the age group 6-17 years in 1974-75. Numerically speaking, it was certainly an achievement as compared to some 26 million children in school in 1951. The unfortunate fact, however, remained that, there were millions of children without any schooling. Added to them were the millions who dropped out without completing the full education. Thus, 60 per cent children, a very large number in class I itself, dropped out before completing class V and about 75 per cent before completing class VII.

The phenomenal wastage in elementary education has been with our system of education for a long time. The rate of school dropout varied from State to State and within a State, from district to district and from community to community (Chikermane, 1968). For instance, the incidence was much higher among the scheduled castes and backward communities and in the lower age groups, with largest in standard I (Jayaraman, 1967). The staggering proportion of dropouts, on the one hand, rendered the fulfilment of the constitutional objective rather impossible and, on the other,

---

* See Note at the end of the Chapter.

made the system of school education dysfunctional and contra-productive. It was quite natural, therefore, that the attention of educationists and researchers was drawn to the problem of wastage in education. A number of studies conducted on wastage certainly indicated some concern for this important problem. However, over the years, survey after survey, conducted from State to State, has tended to repeat itself. A perusal of these studies (See Appendix to this Chapter) makes this clear. Besides, three other important points are suggested by these studies : (1) As the number of studies on wastage increase, the actual wastage in education also tended to increase (i.e. the studies failed to contribute to reduction in wastage); (2) Although there were a large number of recommendations as to what should be done to reduce wastage, there was no appreciable effort to reduce and control this malady (incidentally, this shows that recommendations alone cannot solve problems); and (3) The suggested causes and the remedies were too fragmented – someone coming out with one cause, another with another cause – without putting these causes in a comprehensive conceptual perspective. The various suggested causes (fragmented and scattered in the various surveys) tended to fall in a conceptual model which could help us understand the problem of wastage in education in a proper perspective. Such an understanding could also help us in devising suitable interventions and educational programmes for universalizing elementary education and in radical social transformation. Such a model is seen in Figs. 2.1, 2.2 and 2.3. We discuss below some of the salient aspects of this conceptual model.

2.2. Causes of Wastage in Education

Poverty

Several studies found poverty as the principal cause of school dropout. The proportions of dropouts were much higher among the poorer communities; in the rural areas as compared to urban areas; and among the scheduled castes and tribes than the traditional higher castes. Out of 100 children, 25 completed elementary education and 10 completed secondary education. Out of the 10 "survivors," eight came from the upper 30 per cent of the society. The remaining two survivors belonged to the "poorer" majority of people (Naik, 1975a). It was quite clear that poverty

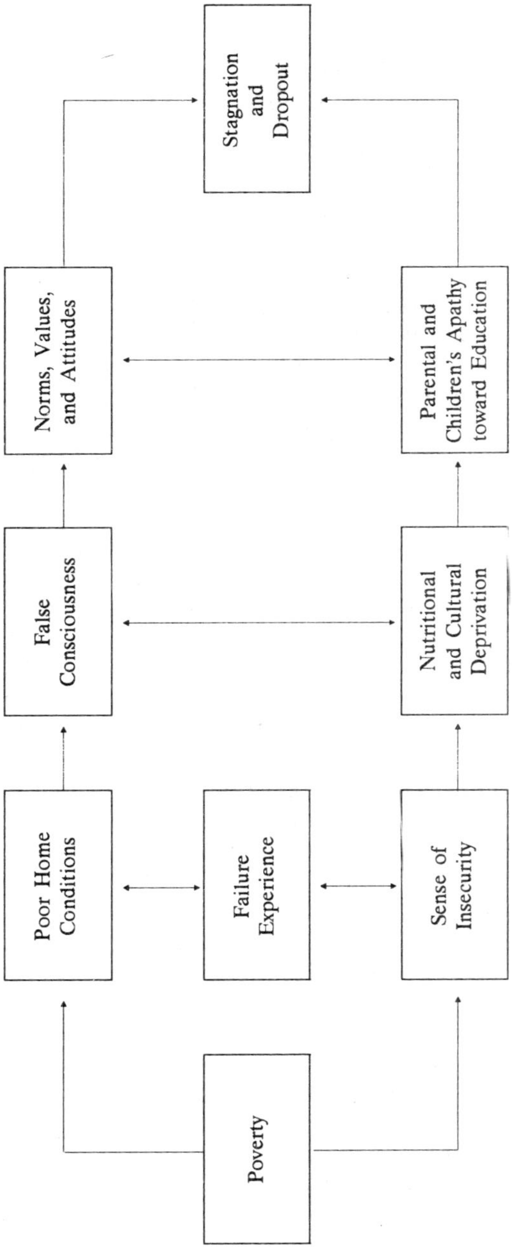

FIG. 2.1 : Socio-Economic Causes of Wastage in Education

prevented children from enrolling in schools, and it also drove them out of the school. A UNESCO (1975) study has established a close correlation between the two. In the 25 least developed countries, where the per capita product was less than $100 a year, illiteracy rates were over 80 per cent. The socio-economic conditions of poverty operated through a series of other variables to cause the "dependent" dropout behaviour among the children. Some such variables, as seen in Fig. 2.1, are described below:

Poor Home Conditions : The most direct consequence of poverty is reflected in poor home conditions of the children. They suffer, as briefly discussed in Chapter 5, from lack of food, clothing, shelter, medical facilities and so on. Parents are mostly engaged in the grim "battle" for physical survival. They have to work all the time to make both ends meet. Thus, children grow up under extremely deprived conditions. They are forced to enter the labour market very early in their childhood in order to earn their bread for the day and to supplement the meagre income of the family.

Failure Experience : Centuries of exploitation and poverty not only give rise to destitute home conditions but also cripple the people's morale. In their pursuit of livelihood, they often experience helplessness and failures. They live under a constant sense of insecurity in the world dominated by their powerful adversaries. They internalize self-doubts, vague fears and negative self-concept. They become sceptical, indifferent and withdrawn.

Sense of Insecurity : The sense of insecurity is passed on to young children. They have fear of eviction from huts and land by the landlord, fear of starvation, fear of facing cold without clothes and fear of all kinds of indignities and humiliations. Children are exposed to such insecurity right from their birth. Such children bring with them this sense of insecurity to the school.

Nutritional and Cultural Deprivation : A direct consequence of poverty and poor home conditions is that children are deprived of proper nutrition. Nutritional deprivation may produce mental retardation in extreme cases and in others weakening of mental faculties. It is a well-known fact that protein deficiency leads to weakening of general mental ability. Along with nutritional deprivation, the poor home conditions inevitably result in "cognitive deprivation." The deprived children lag behind in language development and in learning of various concepts and symbols. Research has established that adverse home conditions depress the IQ by 10 to 15 points in such children. (Bloom *et al.*, 1965).

False Consciousness : The rural poor live in the context of the landlord, moneylender and other powerful elements in the neighbourhood. They are socialized by this powerful social influence over them. They, thus, learn the values and the beliefs taught to them by their masters and exploiters. For instance, they learn that they are born poor and would die poor because of their misdeeds in the past life; that it is their moral duty to submit to the dictates of the landlord and the moneylender who are their masters. Such false consciousness (about their life conditions and poverty and other social issues) work as internalized fetters on them, forcing them to submit to exploitation and domination.

Norms, Values and Attitudes : One of the pernicious effects of false consciousness is the learning of norms, values and attitudes which operate against their own self and class interest and against their liberation from bondage. They learn that education is not for them; they can never be educated as they are incompetent and good for nothing; education or no education – their lot is going to remain the same; it is futile to send children to school because they are born to toil, live and die in poverty.

Apathy Towards Education : One of the consequences of deprivation and false consciousness, operating through entrenched norms and values, is the inculcation of negative attitudes and apathy towards education. The parents show lack of interest in their children's education. Same is the case with children themselves. They perceive education as unimportant.

Fragmented Causes and a Comprehensive Model

The socio-economic system, which breeds, perpetuates and feeds on poverty, is one of the most important inhibiting factors in the universalization of education. It is futile to talk of parental and children's apathy towards education in isolation of certain important socio-economic variables which really cause such an apathy. The same is true of parental fears and insecurity as well as for the need for children to start work early in life. Study after study has found children withdrawn from school so that they could do domestic and/or some other "gainful" work. Part and apparent "causes" are, therefore, not the real causes of school dropout. These can be understood only in a proper conceptual perspective, as seen in Fig. 2.1. Any meaningful policy for dealing with the problem of wastage shall have to reckon with these inter-related social variables. We will come back to this later in this chapter.

2.3. Psycho-Cultural and Educational Causes

The "Elitist" System of Education

Studies and investigations have repeatedly identified certain important educational and psycho-cultural causes of educational wastage. Like the socio-economic factors, these are also inter-related, as seen in Fig. 2.2. As could be expected, most studies picked up some of the well-known aspects of the education system as the source of recurring wastage. These can best be understood in relation to each other and in the perspective of total situation.

The purposes for which the present system of education was introduced by the colonial regime are no longer relevant. The single-entry admission, sequential promotion, full-time courses with full-time teachers, high load of "verbal" content and the strong link with white-collar government employment have converted education into a system of producing, reproducing and reinforcing elitism. The down filtration theory (Naik, 1975) never became operational with the result that we are now faced with the tremendous problem of mass illiteracy in the country. Over the years, the system has been operated for producing urban-based elites (who remain largely unemployed) and large-scale educational wastage (mostly in rural areas). We discuss below some important inputs of this "waste-producing system."

Curriculum and Textbooks

Studies have repeatedly found irrelevant curriculum and textbooks as one of the important causes of educational wastage. The curriculum was either too loaded and/or it was not at all meaingful, particularly for the socially and culturally deprived children. The textbooks were biased towards culturally advantaged children (Rath, 1974). The disadvantaged and deprived children generally did not follow and appreciate such textbooks. Such materials did not meet with their field of experience, and thus reinforced their lack of interest in school. The same is also true of the over-emphasis on English in some urban schools. Such curriculum

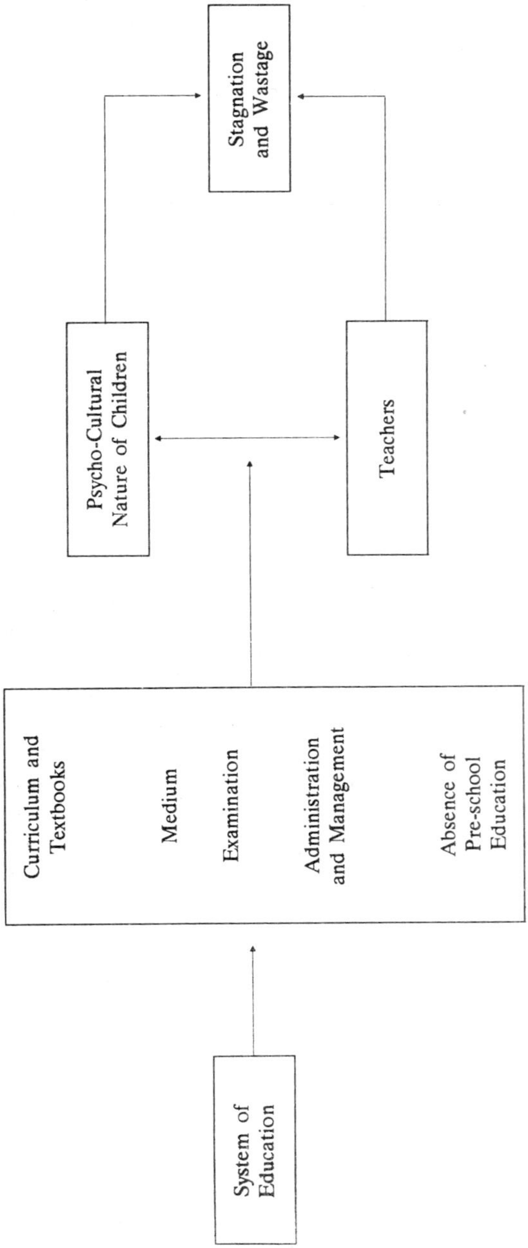

FIG. 2.2 : Psycho-Cultural and Educational Causes of Wastage in Education

and textbooks accentuate feelings of alienation in poverty-striken children. Thus, socially irrelevant and experientially not meaningful curriculum and books become a powerful source of their alienation and demotivation.

Unsuitable Medium of Instruction

Coupled with irrelevant curriculum and biased textbooks, the non-mother tongue medium of instruction made it doubly difficult for the "deprived" children to appreciate the classroom lessons. For tribal and other categories of economically and culturally backward children, the medium of instruction could be a strong cause of their lack of interest in the school. Why should children sit for lessons which they do not follow? This may further accentuate their feeling that school was alien to them; that they did not belong there.

Examination System : Cause of Demotivation

One of the astonishing phenomenon in the Indian education system is, that, the traditional system of examination has continued to rule the scene despite its unanimous condemnation. A system of examination devised under the colonial regime for certain purposes then has not only continued but further increased its entrenched power of directing the teaching-learning efforts. Such examinations are outside the realm of experience of millions of children from poorer homes. Passing or failing children has become the "business" of the system of examination. This system is a powerful source of reinforcement of failure experience of poorer children. No wonder that study after study has found this system of examination as one of the most important reasons for demotivation and wastage in education and for the dropout from schools.

Outmoded Administration and Management

Like the outmoded curriculum and irrelevant textbooks, the outmoded system of school administration has not only continued but is now much more widely entrenched. An "officious" approach to education promotes wastage not only in education but also in the administrative efforts. Problems like large classes; overcrowding in single-teacher schools; herding together of children of different ability levels in one class with one teacher; even without a teacher (as the teacher is absent not very infrequently); children having to walk long distances without any transport facility; lack of minimum instructional and play materials in the school; the indifferent attitude of education officers to such issues – all these and more interact to make the school an unattractive place for children to go to. An unsuitable school administration and mismanagement greatly reduce efficiency of the school system as a whole. Lack of efficient management of school system and lack of imagination prevented identification and utilization of local resources – human and physical – for benefit of the children. This is much more true of the urban poor and rural areas where most illiteracy and school dropout exist.

Paucity of Pre-school Education

The home conditions of the large majority of poor children is not conducive to their adequate cognitive development in their early formative years (Deutsch *et al.*, 1968). In the absence of adequate cognitive and motivational development at home and in the absence of pre-school education, we can understand the fate of such children in class I in the school. No wonder that the largest dropout occurs in class I itself. The poorer children are not able to cope with some of the tasks needed for this stage of education.

The existing pre-school education is loaded in favour of urban children from educated homes. The costly urban pre-primary education cannot be replicated for the whole country. How can meaningful experience be provided to poorer rural children in the age group up to six years without proper interventions and adequate funds?

The above-mentioned systemic variables, as seen in Fig. 2.2, are all inter-related. Interacting among themselves, they have the potential of playing havoc with the system of education, particularly with the education of children from economically poor households. The other two important blocks of variables interacting with the system are related to children themselves and their teachers.

Psycho-Cultural Nature of Children

As already mentioned above, socio-economic variables contribute to both nutritional and cognitive deprivation of children. Besides lack of adequate and desired mental preparedness, some of the cultural artifacts of deprivation hinder such children in the classroom.

Teachers Hold the Fate

By any criterion, teachers hold the fate of education in their hands. Children are entrusted to their care. Several studies have found teachers in primary schools not qualified for the jobs they held; they were paid poorly; they were highly discontented and frustrated. They showed lack of love and affection for children from the lower castes. The teaching was highly punishment-oriented. Such alienated teachers, interacting with socio-economically deprived and probably alienated children, contributed little to universalizing education.

2.4. Interaction Among Socio-Economic and Educational Variables

An education system does not exist in vacuum. It is an institution of the larger social system with which it constantly interacts. It is an integral part of its power structure. As several studies conducted during the 1960s, 1970s and before showed, socio-economic factors, as discussed above, interact with and influence educational variables, as seen in Fig. 2.3. Home conditions interact with school conditions. The teacher's values, norms and attitudes and her/his expectation of the poor deprived children are reinforced by false consciousness of the parents and children themselves. The teacher's own sense of insecurity combines with the children's sense of insecurity and fear of failure. Wastage in education, and school dropout have, therefore, to be understood as dependent variables, as seen in Fig. 2.3.

Thus, universalization of education was greatly hampered by a large-scale dropout. Programmes for universalization of elementary education were based on weak ground where basic socio-economic variables continued to impede it. As a result, elementary education—even basic literacy—got denied to a large majority of our people.

2.5. Elementary Education in the 1970s and 1980s

There has not been much improvement in the elementary education situation during the 1970s and 1980s as has been brought

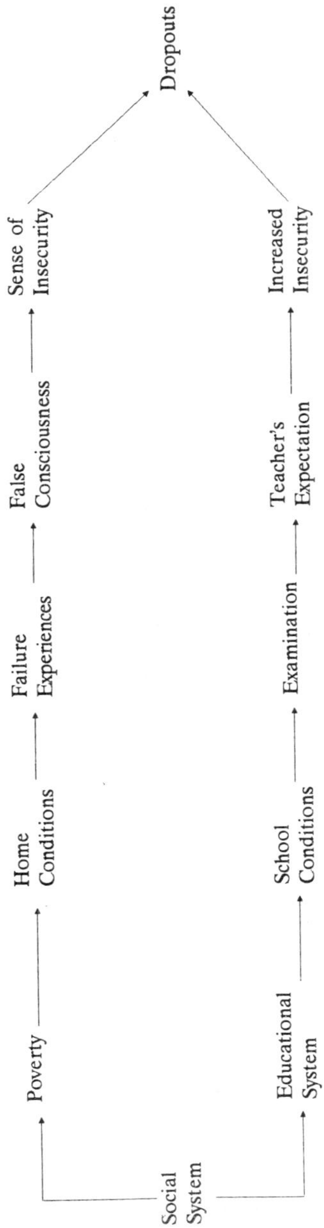

FIG. 2.3 : Socio-Economic and Educational Variables

out in the policy perspective paper (Ministry of Education, 1985) and subsequent official documents (Ministry of Human Resource Development, 1990, 1990a) and by the Committee for the Review of National Policy on Education (NPE), (Ministry of H.R.D., 1990b). Inadequate enrolment, high school – dropout and the poor quality of schooling have continued unabated. Some of the salient characteristics of the situation, as obtained during this period, are briefly summarized below :

Enrolment of Children : Far Short of Target

The enrolment has been lagging behind with wide variations from State to State. The progress in this sector (i.e., universal elementary education) has been far short of the target. In fact, the targets moved farther and farther to accommodate the failure arising from inadequacy of resources or sheer lack of viable strategy. The national aggregate figures were impressive but they hid tremendous disparities between states, sections of society and sexes. The enrolment was as low as 62.9 per cent in Assam. There were districts where enrolment of girls was as low as 17 per cent (Jalore in Rajasthan) while the enrolment of girls on the all-India basis was 75.5 per cent. The overall enrolment position, therefore, was not satisfactory despite the apparent achievements in terms of gross enrolment ratio (Ministry of Education, 1985 : 35).

Growth of Schools and Increase in Teachers

The number of primary schools increased from 209,671 in 1950-51 to 543,677 in 1987-88, thus registering a growth by a quotient of 2.6. During the same period upper primary schools, high schools and colleges of general education taken together increased by a quotient of 9.9. The growth in the number of teachers was almost parallel to the growth in institutions – about threefold in primary school teachers and a quotient of 10.6 in others. The neglect of elementary education was further shown by the fact that 3 out of every 10 primary schools had one teacher (or may be none) and 6 out of 10 had up to two teachers.

Infrastructure Deprivation

The number of schools increased. However, 40 per cent of them were reported to have no pucca buildings; 39.72 per cent did not have a black board and 59.50 per cent had no drinking water. As mentioned above, some 35 per cent of the schools were doing with only a single teacher who was supposed to teach three to four different classes. In fact, some surveys indicated that many schools remained without a teacher for long periods of time. Some teachers were reported to be indulging in sub-contracting teaching work to others who were not qualified for this work, either by training or by experience (*ibid* : 35-36).

Quality of Education

The quality of instructional work could be very well imagined in view of the position regarding the availability of teachers as mentioned above. It was reported that the courses taught in State-run or aided schools were not always related to child environment. New methods of teaching science and mathematics, recommended as essential ingredients of the primary curricula, were being ignored in many States; and most of the schools did not have even the relatively inexpensive teaching kits developed by the NCERT. By and large, the methods of teaching were also quite outmoded. Very often, this encouraged children to memorizing the contents of books and the expected question-answers. The programme of Work Experience or Socially Useful Productive Work had not been implemented in most schools (*ibid* : 36).

Wastage and Dropout

"With such schools and with such teaching and with about 40 per cent of the population living below the poverty line, it is not surprising that the growth rate of enrolment in elementary education tended to taper off" (*ibid* : 36). A large number of those who enrolled very soon dropped out. Of the 100 children enrolled in class I, only 23 reached class VIII. The rest had to be satisfied only with some literacy or they got added to the mass of the illiterates in the country. It must be emphasized that the schools where majority of children, whether in town or in rural areas, studied were far poorer in facilities, quality and relevance of education. As a result, we may be marching into the 21st century with an inacceptably large corpus of illiterate people (*ibid* : 36-37).

Paucity of Funds for Elementary Education

Paucity of resources has been one of the most important reasons for the failure in the elementary education. The total expenditure per student per year by the Centre and the States has tended to decline in real terms. The total expenditure on education increased from 1.2 per cent of the GNP in 1950-51 to about 4 per cent 1986-87. Expenditure on elementary education also increased from Rs. 850 million in 1951-56 (First Plan period) to Rs. 28,490 million in 1985-90 (Seventh Plan period). This increase, however, did not keep pace with the increase in the prices and student population. As a result, we are spending either the same or a lower amount per student than in the 1950s and 1960s (Ministry of HRD, 1990b). More than 90 per cent of the funds (in some States even more than 98 per cent) was spent on teachers' salaries and administration. Practically, nothing was available to buy black boards and chalks let alone charts and other inexpensive teaching aids or even pitchers for drinking water (Ministry of Education, 1985).

Progress of Elementary Education

The New Education Policy—1986, resolved to ensure that all children who attained the age of 11 years by 1990 will have had five years of schooling or its equivalent through non-formal education (NFE). Likewise, it was resolved that by 1995 all children up to 14 years of age would be provided free and compulsory education (Ministry of HRD, 1986 : 12). This policy promised universalization of elementary education by 1990. It was expected that of the additional 64 million children coming up for elementary education, nearly 39 million would be educated entirely through NFE (Ministry of Education, 1985 : 64).

The above goals were to be achieved by providing essential facilities to primary schools : supplying them improved learning materials; applying modern technological aids; improving learning environment of NFE centres; by improved selection and training of teachers and by using improved curriculum.

It is, however, not yet known, through any systematic study, as to how far non-formal education could be effective in fulfilling the basic objective of nurturing cognitive development, national pride and integration and cultural cohesion in children and in facilitating internalization of democratic values in them. However, the Committee for the Review of National Policy on Education came to the conclusion that half the children in the age group of 6-14 years either did not enter school at all or dropped out at an early stage. About one-third to one-half found the school either boring and irrelevant or threatening. Another 40 to 45 per cent stayed away from school due to economic compulsions and the demands for households and family life. Only about 5 per cent of the children managed to reach the higher secondary stage and a small percentage went on to higher education (Ministry of HRD, 1990b).

2.6. Adult Education and Functional Literacy

The failure in elementary education has directly contributed to mass illiteracy in the country. In absolute numbers, there were 437 million illiterates in the country in 1981 against 300 million at the time of independence. Adult literacy in rural areas varied from 64.7 per cent in Kerala to 5.5 per cent in Rajasthan. In Bihar, Madhya Pradesh and Uttar Pradesh, which accounted for 38 per cent of the rural families in the country, the female literacy percentage ranged between 8.99 and 10.17 as assessed in 1981. A UNESCO study has revealed that the adult literacy level of 70 per cent is a critical threshold for universalization of elementary education. Illiterate parents are prone to avoid enrolling their children and to taking them out if it meant any inconvenience (Ministry of Education, 1985 : 41-42).

The "Demand" for Education

Thus, elementary education continued to suffer from various structural, administrative and instructional blocks all these years since independence. The enrolment itself has been low. This is further compounded by a high dropout rate. Macro-economic problems, increasing unemployment and lack of income coupled with social backwardness of the people bring down education in their priorities of life. They do not perceive mere literacy and elementary education as important in their battle for survival. Concerted efforts to organize them and to involve them in the mass movement for education and better life do help them to appreciate the need for education (Mehta, 1990; 1992). Such heightened awareness and interest might put "demand" on the system of education, and somewhat activize it. Creation of an active "demand" for education in the thoughts of the people on the one hand, and planned socio-educational interventions on the other could give a decisive push towards its universalization (see Chapters 8 and 9 for further discussion).

2.7. Interventions for Universalizing Education

Need for Rethinking and Action

By and large, most States are now providing free and/or subsidized textbooks and some other educational materials like slates and pencils. Some states are also providing free mid-day meals to needy children in primary schools. These are important measures for attracting children to school and for enabling them to continue education. These are, however, admittedly not enough. The poorer children are eliminated very early in the race and the fruits of education continue to go to the rich. Thus, fulfilment of the constitutional objective has continued to elude us. It is time, therefore, that we think afresh, devise and implement more effective interventions to bring about universalization of education.

"We Recommend and You Act"

One interesting tendency emerges from the various published studies of wastage in education as well as from the reports of various committees and commissions (see studies in the Appendix of the end the Chapter). It is the *separation* of recommendation from action. There has been a plethora of committee "advice" and recommendations as to how wastage in education should be curtailed and how elementary education should be universalized. The situation seems to be characterized by "we recommend and you act" and "recommend but don't act." Some recommendations have addressed to other agencies such as teachers for being put into action. Actors such as teachers have seldom been involved in thinking about problems and in making of the recommendations. There is a split between promise and practice and between recommendations and policy. The situation is analogous to the split in education itself—one for "haves" and the other for "have-nots." Such a system divides life into watertight compartments – one having the benefit of full-time education and no work and the other of full-time work and no education (Ministry of Education, 1976 : 8). Such dichotomies have important correlates some of which are discussed below.

Bureaucratic vs. Development Approach

The problem of wastage in education and the national goal of universalizing education can hardly be tackled and achieved by a bureaucratic approach. "Part of the reason" as identified in the critical appraisal for the New Education Policy, "for such a situation is an undeniable fact that the school system has become a gigantic bureaucratic set-up leaving no room for interventions at the local levels" (Ministry of Education, 1985 : 39). Education is an important developmental activity. Like other such activities, it needs a developmental approach with a movement from *paper to action* in the field. The single-entry sequential system of education foisted by the colonial rulers and further strengthened since independence is in itself an example of the bureaucratic system. There is no wonder that officers manning the departments of education are rigid in their functioning.

The objective of universalizing education is antithetic to elitist control of education. Development of people at the grassroot level through universal education is bound to bring about a radical transformation of the rural scene which has been dominated by superstitition for a long time. Such an important task cannot be performed and fulfilled by the existing bureaucratically oriented education departments and other related government agencies. There is a need to decentralize educational administration along with the system of administering social change and development programmes. It is essential for promoting large-scale participation of the people themselves in the task of organizing and energizing education for them (Mehta, 1990). Mass mobilization and involvement of the people in this process can itself become an instrument of education. Participation of people is, however, not possible without broadening the base of administration and its democratization (Pareek, 1989; Mehta, 1989).

Education vs. Failing

The system of education has long been blamed for large-scale failures at examinations. Year after year, may be for more than the past 100 years, almost 50 per cent of all those who took secondary examination failed. Such large-scale failure has become an integral part of the system of education (Passi, 1974). As mentioned above, due to various historical and socio-economic reasons, our people have accumulated failure experiences and internalized a fear of failure and insecurity. Large-scale deprivation and ruthless exploitation under which the country's poor have been living for a long time perpetuate such learning and prevent them from trying to break the stranglehold of the system on them. The education system further reinforces the same failure experience in their children. There is a *basic* difference between *educating* and *failing*. Despite large-scale failures, the quality of education has hardly improved. Detaining the child and preventing him/her from going ahead cannot be considered as an act of education. It certainly does not help the poor child to achieve what he needs so desperately—success experience. Education has to be elevated from being a mere class room ritual to becoming an important social process. It has to move from being a single-shot lottery (pass-fail) to becoming a learning process for social and individual development.

Teacher Training and Mobilization of Resources

As mentioned above, several studies have found inadequacy of teaching and lack of qualified teachers as the cause of stagnation and wastage in education. Teacher education is a continuous process and the system (of teacher education) needs to be overhauled as was recognized in the New Education Policy (Ministry of HRD 1986 : 36). Looking to the tremendous nature of the problem, it is very doubtful whether we would be able to provide adequately trained full-time professional teachers following traditional methods for our primary schools. This will necessitate a fresh look at the teacher training programmes and also readiness to draw upon our own experiments in education for the purpose of enriching theories of teaching and learning.

One of the important psychological causes of stagnation and wastage was the attitude of teachers toward children from the scheduled castes and other backward communities. Teachers generally do not expect much from such children and don't fail to convey this expectation to the children. They loudly "predict" that such children would not be able to complete their education; that they would either fail or dropout; that such children cannot learn mathematics or such other subjects; that how they learn when their parents have not seen even the face of a book. Such attitudes and expectations tend to become self-fulfilling. Teachers behave in such discouraging ways that their predictions are "proved" correct. In fact "dropouts" further strengthen the teachers' low and derogatory perceptions.

The Education Commission (1964-66) (Ministry of Education, 1966) had talked of the need for maximum utilization of human resources for the development of education. The meagre resources are misutilized due to inefficiency in the system of education. This is largely due to structural problems which tend to weaken motivation and lower commitment among the teachers and administrators. Experiments conducted in motivating teachers suggest that suitably designed programmes could develop motivation which in turn might become an important source of increased efficiency leading to an overall improvement in academic performance of both teachers and their pupils. These are, however, shortlived gains which tend to taper off in absence of proper structural support (Mehta, 1976). It is essential, therefore, to pay attention to the working and living conditions of teachers, to the system of educational administration and to teacher education in a comprehensive way.

Irrelevant Curriculum and Books

As already mentioned, the disadvantaged child finds the present curriculum and books in a primary school not only irrelevant, but loaded against him/her. They are mostly based on the experience pattern of culturally and economically better-off children. An important educational principle of children's learning, i.e., the *curriculum should be new but not so new* (Hunt, 1968, 1973; Piaget, 1952; Jensen, 1968) is grossly violated here. The curriculum appears to be largely unfamiliar. The textbooks are largely alien to the field of experience of the socio-economically and culturally deprived children. There is a need, therefore, to take a hard look at the entire process of curriculum and textbook development. The content and concepts, the curricular mix and load, the methodology of presentation, integration of life experience with newer materials – all these need attention in classroom lessons.

Ad-hoc Attempts vs. Institutional Development

The studies surveyed in this paper have reported various kinds of ad-hoc recommendations and some ad-hoc attempts at improving the situation of primary education. The various state governments have introduced some such recommended practices. For example, the introduction of three-hour school; provision of women teachers for rural schools; conversion of some single- teacher schools into multi-teacher schools. These are useful attempts as far as they go. But such ad-hoc attempts hardly meet the need for fulfilling the constitutional task of universalizing education.

We have been conditioned for a long time to think of education as a system of classroom teaching for carrying out the formalized instructional process. Several ad-hoc attempts have been tried in the context of such a concept of traditional institution. But the extraordinary task of educating the millions in the country cannot be carried out by the outmoded agency of that traditional school institution. There is a need for bringing about a radical transformation of the institution of education. For this, we may have to use all kinds of educational practices – from classroom to open-door mass campaigns and people's movements, from full-time teachers to self-study, from sequential system of education to multiple entry system of education. In this respect, creative institution building capable of implementing the national goal of universal education needs urgent attention.

2.8. Some Notable Interventions

During the past few years, some notable attempts have been initiated toward innovative institution-building. It is now realized that mass literacy is linked inseparably with the problem of universalization of elementary education. It is also being increasingly realized that illiteracy cannot be wiped out in isolation of certain urgent socio-economic changes. In fact, the World Literacy Movement is getting geared to consider campaigns for literacy as important instruments of radical social transformation (Ministry of Education, 1975). In the past some years, some significant attempts have been initiated to intervene and accelerate the tempo of universal education, mass literacy and socio- economic development (Ministry of Education, 1975; Ministry of HRD, 1988). By way of historical perspective and learning experience, we examine below two such interventions which attracted attention at the time of their implementation in the 1970s.

Farmers' Training and Functional Literacy

Several attempts have been made from time to time to make non-formal education a component of larger developmental programmes. The Farmers' Functional Literacy Programme (FFLP) was a good illustration of such efforts. It was one of the 10 largest single country-wide programmes of non-formal education. This Central Government scheme was implemented in a hundred selected agricultural districts during the Fourth Plan and 70 more districts were to be added in the Fifth Plan. "The basic assumption underlying the project is that there is a direct correlation between development and education and that material resource inputs must be accompanied by human resource inputs to realize development objective." (Ministry of Education, 1973 : 8).

The FFLP sought to help the Green Revolution; bring about socio- economic changes; and to accelerate the acquisition of literacy skills. Most of the respondents were in the age-group 15 to 25 years and were small land holders possessing three or less acres of land. We know that the Green Revolution took place mostly with the help of large farms and in such populations who could afford the use of improved seed, fertilizer and other practices (Pai, 1976). It is, therefore, not clear as to how such poor farmers, who were forced to engage in other secondary occupations for earning their livelihood, were involved in a project for accelerating the Green Revolution. The literacy programme also sought to increase knowledge of high-yielding variety of wheat and adoption of improved seed, fertilizers, implements and insecticides. One of the achievements, as reported in this functional literacy programme, was an increase in the possession and use of material goods by the respondents. Their exposure to radio and newspapers also increased. It was amazing how the marginal and land-poor farmers could buy materials and goods without having adequate income. Although not mentioned, the data tended to suggest that, irrespective of the stated target group, the project population and the respondents in the study came from the better-off section of the village population. In fact, it is a well-known fact that the extension strategy designed to promote adoption of improved seeds and fertilizers largely benefit only the rich farmers (Mehta, 1991). Since the FFLP also adopted a similar extension strategy along with some literacy inputs, it was likely to benefit mostly the rich farmers.

There was, however, nothing wrong in helping rich farmers to attain literacy and also to adopt improved practices. This was likely to help production of high-yielding crops. What was, however, not clear, but implicit, was the impact of such a programme on the landless and land-poor sections of the people in the same district (Pai, 1976). Over the decade of 1960s, the proportion of agricultural labour tended to increase and the number of cultivators went down with concentration of land holdings in the hands of a few (Census, 1971). More and more village people joined the ranks of wage labourers during this period suggesting their increasing pauperization. The dynamics of such rural development, therefore, resulted in the widening of the gap between the rich and the poor. In such an agrarian situation, it was doubtful if the Lucknow project could be replicated among the marginal farmers and rural labour. As is known, the largest dropout from primary schools occurs among the children from such poor homes. A functional literacy project for the rich farmers was, therefore, not likely to promote universalization of elementary education and much less, socio-economic development of the rural poor.

Bhumiadhar Non-formal Education Project

Some of the shortcomings of the farmers' literacy programme were sought to be remedied by another project sponsored by the Ministry of Education in 1970 at Bhumiadhar in Nainital District of Uttar Pradesh (NCERT, 1976). Bhumiadhar was selected for the project in view of its poverty. Some 250 scheduled caste families and about a hundred school dropouts in the age group of 6 to 14 years were identified there. The land was not fertile and there was an acute scarcity of water. Majority of the people were labourers. They travelled about 10 km for their daily wage work. Poverty was the main cause of the children's dropout from the school.

The non-formal education project was sponsored in order to : (i) enable the school dropout to again join the regular stream, either in class VI or class IX in formal schools, and (ii) bring about some socio-economic changes in the community. The project carried out several activities and interventions such as the following : barren land was tilled; improved variety of seed tried out; skills imparted to the community for cultivating mushroom; 40 compost pits prepared; *vanmahotsav* observed : campaign launched for health education; launching of ceramics, tie-and-dye and papier-mache; production of fruit juice, jelly and jams; promotion of stitching, sewing, poultry, rope- and net-weaving; and cattle rearing for increased milk production. Some of these operations yielded products on commercial basis. The organizers thought that, "as the members of the community are labourers and are illiterate, they are not in a position to think of ways and means of improving their socio- economic conditions," (NCERT, 1976 : 11). It was necessary, therefore, to invite a group of experts from various fields for developing such products and to train the villagers in the process.

Their report is silent about the ownership of the land tilled with the help of experts as the respondents were mostly rural labourers. Studies conducted during the same period in Bihar, Orissa and other States (Maharaj and Iyer, 1975; Iyer and Das, 1976; Das, 1976) showed that such labourers got a daily wage ranging from Rs. 2 to 4.50 or in lieu 1 to 1.5 kg of some coarse grain. They possessed hardly any belongings and lived constantly from hand to mouth. They were forced into indebtedness and, may be, some of them into becoming bonded labourers. The economic situation of rural labourers in the Nainital District of Uttar Pradesh could not have been different (RBI, 1972). Under such socio-economic conditions, introduction of a variety of agro-industrial products, such as those mentioned above, for the benefit of the rural poor was very interesting as these were more likely to benefit the rural rich. In view of the nature of the infrastructure needed for the products introduced, it was quite likely that the rich would dominate such activities.

Work Experience and Non-formal Education

It was not clear how the work experience, relating to the products mentioned above, was meaningful for the school dropouts in the age group of 6 to 14 years – the targets of this project. How did this help them to make good the loss due to their leaving the school and how would such literacy help them to enter class VI and IX in the formal school – the main objective of the project? How could children, "taught" in such a non-formal way through quite a different curriculum, be integrated once again in the traditional programme of formal school? Such questions remained unanswered in the project.

"Expert-Meeting" Approach to Development

The project provided an interesting illustration of an "officious" approach to education and development. As the people were "ignorant," expert meetings had to be called. The talk of teacher being the key to all development was belied by the pattern of project expenditure. An amount of Rs. 27,000 was spent on the meeting of experts, whereas a sum of only Rs. 1,000 was to be used in the entire year on a part-time teacher (NCERT, 1976). It was quite clear that the experts were running the project and not the teachers and certainly not the people concerned. This "expert-meeting" approach to non-formal education and to socio-economic transformation could produce reports, not development. From the outset, the project was not designed to provide education to the poor, neither parents nor their children, and much less their socio-economic development. It was addressed more to the rich. Planned interventions including organization and self-action were needed for the education of the poor, as discussed in Chapter 9.

Organizing Rural Labour

During the same period when the Bhumiadhar NFE project was being implemented, efforts were initiated by the National Labour Institute to organize and educate the rural poor. A series of rural labour camps and related training and educational activities were conducted to involve people in their own development (for reports of such camps, see NLI, 1984). Some such educational efforts are discussed in Chapter 6. The World Literacy Movement tended to move in this direction with an increasing emphasis on developing capability of assertion among the illiterate people (Ministry of Education, 1975). The literacy programme by drawing people to participate in movements and in self-action development and organizational activities could promote and reinforce their sense of social and personal efficacy (Mehta, 1976b; 1983; 1994a) and their need for social achievement (Mehta, 1994), as discussed in Chapters 8 and 9.

The same is true of workers' education and workers' participation. Non-formal training of workers and their participation in management (Mehta, 1976a; 1976b) could help promote in them democratic consciousness and a sense of efficacy. Research on participation (Pateman, 1970; Blumberg, 1968; Mehta, 1976c; 1976b; 1981, 1983, 1993a) show that adults who participate in civic/political activities have a higher sense of political efficacy as well as allegiance to democratic values.

Mobilization of the rural people, including eligible children for social transformation and their active participation in such movements, is likely to enhance their social awareness, critical consciousness and sense of efficacy and assertion (see Chapters 8 and 9). Such mobilization and movements would enhance the need and demand for universalizing education. The foremost task is to pay attention to the totality of the situation and to develop a comprehensive programme. This could include projects for mobilization, awareness and organization; socio-economic projects; employment generation; skill development, literacy and children's education. Grassroot-level field workers and the people themselves have contributed some valuable insights towards such movements for education and development (Mehta, 1990, 1992).

2.9. Education and Social Transformation

Self-action programmes could initiate movement towards education and development. The people are capable of acting to free themselves from the exploiters and moneylenders (see Chapter 8 and 9). Such efforts help develop self-esteem and release aspiration for mobility and better life among the people (see Chapter 3). Education has an important role in this process. For example, there are laws for payment of minimum wages and abolition of bonded labour. Such laws have existed for quite some time. However, the practice of bonded labour like several other pernicious and illegal social and economic practices, has continued unabated (Sharan, 1976; Mehta, 1993b). The people are largely ignorant of such important national policies and social laws which are supposed to safeguard their dignity and freedom. In fact, efforts at educating them about such Acts and their rights are met with stiff resistance of the privileged and powerful entrenched vested interests (see Chapter 8).

Thus, education should make the people not only conscious but also capable of asserting on their environment so that it could be transformed for a better life for themselves. There can be no distinction between formal and non-formal education as far as this important objective is concerned. With an enhanced sense of personal and social efficacy, and a sense of assertion, the people would "demand" education for themselves and for their children. Active participation in movements for education and development would further strengthen their consciousness and efficacy. In this social learning and educational process, the illiterate people would not only attain literacy but also develop various technical and social skills and motivation needed for socio-economic activities. Such socio-educational interventions could, thus, help release productive capabilities of our people for an all-round development of the society (Mehta, 1994a). Some aspects of such educational and developmental efforts are discussed in subsequent chapters.

Note

This chapter is presented in three sections. Section I contains a paper presented at a seminar held at the National Council of Educational Research and Training in November, 1976. This was later published as a paper entitled 'Socio-Psychological Interventions for Universalizing Education (*Vikalpa*, 1977, 2(1), 59-73). The first part of this paper is reproduced in Section I in order to present a historical perspective.

Section II presents a review of the status of elementary education a decade later i.e., in 1985-86. It includes some portions of a paper entitled "Education Oriented Development Strategy : Universalisation of Elementary and Adult Education" presented at a seminar on New Education Policy held in September, 1985.

Section III contains a discussion of interventions for universalising education and for release of productive energy of the people. It also provides some linkage with some other chapters of the book.

APPENDIX I

SOME SURVEYS ON WASTAGE

Amrutham, M.S.V., "The Problem of Early-School Leavers and Droup-outs," *Educational Review*, LXXIX (4), April 1973, pp. 84-85.

Battacharyya, S., "Wastage and Stagnation in Education," *Bulletin of the West Bengal Headmasters' Association*, 17(1), 1968, pp. 3-7.

Bhatt, C.S., "Impact of Three Hours' Schools on Enrolment Wastage of and Stagnation in Rajasthan," *Educational India*, 36(11-12), 1970, pp. 370-74.

Bose, A.K., "Wastage in Secondary Education," *Educational Review*, 75(3), 1969, pp. 60-64; 75(2), 1970, pp. 259-62; 76(1), 1971, pp. 18-20; 76(2), 1971, pp. 41-45.

Central Institute of Research and Training in Public Cooperation, *School Dropout among Harijan Children : Causes and Cure*, New Delhi, 1975.

Chaudhary, N.D., "Dropout and Stagnation in a Tribal Situation," *Education Quarterly*, 26(3), October 1974, pp. 25-33.

——, "Educational Development among the Scheduled Tribes in Rajasthan," *Education Quarterly*, 27, October 1975, pp. 26-30.

Chawla, M., "Reduction of Wastage and Stagnation in Secondary Schools," *Teacher Speaks*, 4, 1967, pp. 129- 34.

Chickermane, D.V., "The States' Reports on Wastage and Stagnation : A Study of Wastage in Primary Education," *Education Quarterly*, 20(3), October 1968, pp. 1-13.

——, "A Study of Wastage in Primary Education in India," *Education Quarterly*, 20(3), October 1968, pp. 14-15, 17.

——, "A Study of Wastage in Single Teachers' Schools," *Education Quarterly*, 20(3), October 1968, pp. 22-23.

Chaudhary, P., "Report of an Investigation into the Problem of Wastage and Stagnation in Primary Schools in the District of 24-Parganas," *Education Quarterly*, 20(3), October, 1968, p. 24.

Das, B., "Wastage in Primary School Level," *Orissa Education Magazine*, 11(2), 1967, pp. 47-57.

Das, Ramesh Chandra, "An Investigation into the Problem of Wastage and Stagnation at the Primary Level of Education in the District of Sibsagar," D. Phil Thesis, Gauhati : Gauhati University, 1970.

Desai, K.G., "Guidance for Reducing Wastage in Education," *NIE Journal*, 4(5-6), 1970, pp. 63-65.

Diraviam, K., "Wastage in Education," *New Frontiers in Education*, 3(3), 1973, pp. 12-18.

D'Souza, A.A., "Problem of Wastage in Secondary Education," *Orissa Education Magazine*, 11(3), 1967, pp. 68-70, 81.

Education Commission (1964-66), "Education of Scheduled Tribes," in *Education and National Development*, Delhi : Manager of Publications, 1966, pp. 139- 43, 613-14.

Gill, P.S.; Prasad, B.G.; and Shrivastava, R.N., "Nutritional Status of Primary School Children in a Rural Area of Lucknow," *Indian Journal of Pediatrics*, 35, 1968, pp. 314-26.

Government College of Education, *Wastage and Stagnation in Secondary Education*, Bilaspur : Government College of Education, 1968.

Iyer, R.R., "Wastage in Primary Education," *Education Quarterly*, 20(3), October 1968, pp. 35-46.

Jayaraman, M., *Stagnation and Wastage in Primary Schools*, New Delhi : National Council of Educational Research and Training, 1967.

Jeanne, Periera; and Tirtha, N.V., "A Study of Some Factors Influencing Social Adjustment in Pre-School Children," *Research Bulletin* of the Department of Psychology, Osmania University, 7, 1972, pp. 37-51.

Jorapur, P.B., "Drop-outs in School Education : Rural Conditions Demand Basic Changes," *Yojana*, 14(12), 1970, pp. 19-20.

Kaul, G.N., "Reducing Wastage and Stagnation : An Appraisal and Strategy," *Quest in Education*, 8(4), 1971, pp. 189-93.

Khandekar, Mandakini, *Promoting Socio-Emotional Development of Low-Income Children*, Bombay : Unit for Study of the Urban Child and Youth, Tata Institute of Social Sciences (mimeo).

——, "A Study of Drop-Outs," *Indian Journal of Social Work*, 34(4), 1974, pp. 367-85.

——, "A Study of Drop-Outs" *Indian Journal of Social Work*, 35(1), 1975, pp. 7-19.

Khandekar, Mandakini and Kini, Sushila, "The Social Dimension of Child Nutrition among the Economically Disadvantaged in Greater Bombay," *Social Change*, 4, 1974, pp. 24-35.

Kosh, E.T.; Prasad, R.B.; Jain, V.C.; and Bhushan, Vidya, "A Study on Health of Primary Urban School Children," *Indian Journal of Medical Research*, 58(12), pp. 1742-52.

Lall, D.I., "Problem of Wastage and Stagnations in Haryana," *Haryana Journal of Education*, 1(4), 1968, pp. 20-27.

Leonard, J.P., "Wastage in Education in India," *Indian Educational Review*, 6(9), 1967, pp. 3-9.

Malviya, K.D.; Sen Gupta, J.K.; Shrivastava, R.; and Prasad, B.G., "Nutrition Status of Primary School Children in Some Schools in the Area of Rural Health Training Centre : Sarojini Nagar," *Indian Journal of Public Health*, 13(2), 1969, pp. 71-75.

Muralidharan, R., "Home Stimulation and Child Development," *Indian Educational Review*, 5(2), 1970, pp. 43-51.

Muralidharan, R. and Banerji, Uma, "An Exploratory Study of Intellectual Development of Kindergarten Children in Relation to their Paternal Occupations," *Educational and Psychological Research Journal*, 1(1), 1973, pp. 1-5.

——, "Language Development of Kindergarten Children In Relation to Their Paternal Occupations," *Indian Educational Review*, 8(2), 1973, pp. 1-9.

——, "Effect of Pre-School Education on the Language and Intellectual Development of Underprivilage Children," *Journal of Education and Psychology*, 32(1), 1974, pp. 10- 15.

——, "Effect of Pre-School Education on the School Readiness of Under-privileged Children of Delhi," *Internatio- nal Journal of Early Childhood Review*, 7(2), 1975, pp. 188-92.

Nagappa, S., "Wastage in the Educational System," *Education Quarterly*, 20(3), October 1968, pp. 16-17.

Nagaraj, K.R., "Investigation into Absenteeism in Primary Schools," *Journal of the College of Education*, 5(2), 1967, pp. 53-55.

Patil, M.G., "Guidance and Means of Reducing Wastage and Stagnation of Secondary Schools," *Teacher Speaks*, 4, 1967, pp. 122-8.

Puranik, G.A., "A Study of the Educationally Backward Children in the Age-group 8-12 Years in Nagpur Schools," *Indian Educational Review*, 5(2), 1970, pp. 143-47.

Rao, G. Nageswara; and Tikkiwal, B.D., "An Integrated Approach to the Study of Wastage in a Given Course of Education," *Sankhya*, 288(3-4), 1966, pp. 229-36.

Rath, R., *Teaching-Learning Problems of the Disadvantaged Tribal Children*. The Indian Academy of Applied Psychology, 12th Annual Conference, Utkal University, Bhubaneshwar, 1974.

——, "Personality and Behavioural Problems of Disadvantaged," Lecture delivered at the Post-Graduate Department of Psychology, Utkal University, Bhubaneshwer, 1975.

——, "Problems of Integration of the Disadvantaged to the Mainstream," Lecture delivered at the Post-Graduate Department of Psychology, Utkal University, Bhubaneshwer, 1975.

Rath, R. and Dash, A.S., "Cognitive Effects and Classroom Learning of Culturally Deprived Children in the Primary Schools." Paper presented at the East-West Centre for Cross-Cultural Studies, Honolulu, 1972.

Rawat, D.S., "Draft Blueprint of Action Plan to Reduce Wastage and Stagnation in the Primary and Middle Schools, NCERT, 1975.

"Schools of India," *Education Quarterly*, 20(3), October 1968, pp. 27-34.

Report of the National Seminar on Wastage and Stagation at the Primary Stage, *Education Quarterly*, 20(3), October 1968, pp. 52-57.

Sachidananda, *Structural Constraints in the Education of Scheduled Tribes and Scheduled Castes*, Patna : A.N.S. Institute of Social Studies, 1975.

Safaya, R.N., "Stagnation and Wastage," *Educational Review*, 76(1), 1970, pp. 217-20.

Sapra, C.L., "A Suggested Programme to Reduce Wastage and Stagnation at the First Level of Education," *Education Quarterly*, 20(3), October 1968, pp. 25-26, 57.

——, "Wastage and Stagnation in Elementary Schools" in Mathur, V.S. (ed.), *Crucial Problems in India Education*, Delhi: Arya Book Depot, 1970, pp. 200-18.

Sharma, R.C.; and Sapra, C.L., *Wastage and Stagnation in Primary and Middle Schools in India*, New Delhi : National Council of Educational Research and Training, 1969.

Sharma, R.G., "The Effects of Malnutrition on Mental Growth and Mental Health of the Children," *Indian Journal of Psychiatry*, 15(3), 1973, pp. 272-78.

Singh, Mohindar, and Dosajh, Kanta, "A Study of Stagnation (Failures) In the Primary Schools of Rupar and Kapurthala Districts," *Recent Trends in Education*, 1(1), 1970, pp. 20-22.

Srivastava, Vishnu Swarup, "Environment as a Determining Factor of Failure at High School Stage," *Manas*, 21(1), 1974, pp. 37-42.

Tiwari, Govind Prasad, "Family Dynamic of Drop-outs at the Primary Level," *Indian Psychological Review*, 8(1), 1971, pp. 49-51.

Venkatasubramanian, K., *Constraints of Universalisation of Primary Education and Non-Formal Education*, Material prepared for the use of Task Force on Universalization of Primary Education, New Delhi : NCERT, 1976.

Verma, S.K., "Disadvantaged Children," *Social Welfare*, 16(8), 1969, pp. 13-14.

Vyas, U.K., "Plight of Pre-School Children," *Education Quarterly*, 25(4), January 1975, pp. 22-23.

"Wastage and Stagnation in Primary and Middle Schools in India," NIE-HEW Project 005, Department of Educational Administration, National Council of Educational Research and Training, 1967, *Education Quarterly*, 20-31, October 1968, pp. 18-20.

Zakir, K.L., "Non-Formal Education Programmes in Haryana," *Indian Journal of Adult Education*, 26(11), November 1975, pp. 13-16.

3

YOUTH ASPIRATIONS, EDUCATION AND DEVELOPMENT

AS DISCUSSED in Chapter 2, enrolment in elementary schools has been lagging behind with a large number of children unable to go to school. The high rate of school drop-out has been rendering the entire system ineffective. Under such conditions, it was quite expected that secondary school enrolment would be rather low. Nearly 22 per cent of the students in the age group corresponding to class IX and X were in school during the 1980s. This ratio was in no way near that obtaining in the developed countries (Ministry of Education, 1985 : 43). Secondary education was necessary not only to raise the quality of life of the future citizens but also for improving their potential for productive and creative work. One of the notable but strange historical facts about the system is that almost 50 per cent of all those who took secondary examination in the past more than 100 years have failed each year. Thus, the practice of failure had become an integral part of the system of education (Passi, 1974). One of the most pernicious effects of such widespread dropout and failures was that education, instead of creating a sense of confidence and hope among the children and youth, tended to demoralize and demotivate them for learning.

3.1. Education and Urban Youth

The system of education, thus, has mostly been elite-oriented and has been catering largely to urban youth. Such a system has been marked by some unique socio-psychological characteristics. These in turn shape and promote certain types of youth behaviour with far-reaching implications for the entire society.

Bureaucratic Approach to Change

Since independence, various commissions and committees have made recommendations for changes in the system of education. For instance, several Commissions have repeatedly suggested the need for wide changes in the system of examination as well as in the methods of teaching. Yet, the system has not only continued to function as it was but has become all the more problem-ridden (Ministry of Education, 1985). The Governments, as noted by the Kothari Commission, have been "tinkering with the existing situation and moving forward with faltering steps and lack of faith" (Ministry of Education, 1966 : Foreword). Such a persistent situation, besides being indicative of deeper socio-political factors, has been characterized by separation of recommendations from action and by a split between promise and practice.

Implementation of the suggested educational reforms depended largely on the political will and bureaucratic commitment. Active participation of educational functionaries like Teachers, etc., was also very important for translating recommendations into action in their day-to-day work. In the absence of such a will, commitment and involvement, we have been witnessing a spectacle similar to an epidemic which continues to grow despite correct diagnosis in absence of proper treatment and preventive action (see Chapter 4 for a case study of welfare programmes). The approach to reforming education, like the welfare programmes discussed in Chapter 5, has been casual, bureaucratic and non-professional. The people concerned were hardly involved in analyzing, suggesting and then in implementing the desired changes. There has been practically no attempt to use the vast human resource of parents, teachers and students – the most interested parties in this case – to bring about the desired changes in education.

Education as a Development Activity

The challenge of education is an integral part of the challenge of socio-economic development. For example, universal elementary education and literacy could substantially help in achieving vital social and economic goals of health, skill development, employment and self-action and for transformation of social scene. Universalization would also weaken the urban elite control over education and contribute to social justice, equality and human development. This was, however, not to be and the elementary as well as secondary education have been limping behind, leaving the vast masses of people out and unhelped.

The Changing Character of Higher Education

Higher education in India was expanding at the rate of 10.13 per cent per annum during the 1960s whereas in the developed countries it tended to increase at the rate of 6.6 per cent per annum. It was then estimated that if a 10 per cent rate of expansion per year continued for the next 20 years, enrolment in higher education would be between 7 and 8 million by 1985-86 (UGC, 1971). This rush was probably motivated by rising aspirations among the comparatively disadvantaged sections of society. People, long deprived of education, probably thought that a university degree would pave their way to higher status and better life.

The size of higher education in terms of absolute numbers might have increased over the years because of our population. However, only about 4.8 per cent of the relevant age group was enrolled for higher education during the 1980s. This proportion varied from region to region and was much lower for women, scheduled castes and tribes. A government review of the higher education scene in 1984-85 revealed that, on the whole, the facilities were far below the level of qualitative viability (Ministry of Education, 1985 : 47-48). Combined with an inequitable and slow economic development, the poor quality higher education has contributed to the growing and explosive problem of the educated unemployed. It is an irony of the situation that growing unemployment pushes more and more youth to general courses in our colleges and universities. The set sequence seems to be : no meaningful work/gainful employment – nothing else to do, so why not enrol in a college – a degree may increase employment prospects and/or at least one would feel one is doing something – contributing to more educated unemployment!

3.2. Rising Aspirations and Desire for Participation

In the recent decades, the Indian youth have been exposed to a large number of development programmes, some actual, some promised, including expanding educational opportunities. They have also been subjected to strong populist rhetoric for social justice and better life. In the process, youth aspirations soared, shaping new values and modes of behaviour. As a consequence, there was a significant boost in the demand for students' participation in university decision-making as well as for people's participation in other spheres of life including socio-economic activities. Such youth aspirations have been accompanied by a growing evidence suggesting that participation boosts people's involvement at work, in social movements and in education itself. This view was reflected in the recommendations of the Committee on Governance of Universities when it said "students desire such participation with the object of making education deeper, richer, more meaningful and significant. In other words, the students' desire for participation is founded on academic and not political considerations" (UGC, 1971a : 74).

Experience of Student Participation

Experience with the students' participation in various decision-making bodies of higher education suggested some interesting things. At some universities where representation was given to students on bodies like the Academic Council or even the Syndicate, an agitational posture was carried into such committees. At several places, full-time student activists, who continued to be on the campus for unusually longer periods, succeeded in getting into such committees. At other places, such activists influenced election/nomination of student representatives (on such committees) from outside. There were instances where decisions taken at such university bodies, where student representatives were also present, were opposed and got nullified by other student activists through pressure, threats and agitations. These decisions were concerned with adminissions, examinations, faculty appointments, hostel accommodation, etc. And such issues became the subject matter of agitation (Mehta, 1977).

The decisions taken at appropriate academic and executive bodies were, thus, sought to be reversed outside such bodies under threats of agitations. In this way, the entire decision-making process came under discredit. The rational-legal process tended to lose credibility contributing to a sense of normlessness on the campus. While it was difficult to generalize from such limited experience, it seemed, student activists possessed agitational skills more than such participatory skills as were required for decision-making in the academic bodies. Such a situation also reflected wide-spread and increasing mistrust of university bureaucracy among the students (Mehta, 1977). Agitations yielded greater success under such conditions of mistrust than institutional decision-making processes. May be, the students' sense of powerlessness increased when they sat on joint forums (along with the teachers and others) where there was apparently no power equalization. The student leaders felt much more powerful outside such forums than inside.

Search of Work

A large majority of the country's working population work outside the organized sector of industrial and office work. Almost 70 per cent of them were in the rural workforce, most of whom worked on or around land. Many of them hang around land without any work at all. As is well known, lack of work in villages drives the young rural people to urban areas in search of work.

India's urban population increased by about 50 million during the decade 1971-80. The growth rate was about 46.4 per cent whereas the general population increased by 25 per cent during this period (Census, 1981). In 1977-78, some 38 per cent of the urban population lived below the poverty line (Planning Commission, 1980). It was interesting to know that 75 per cent of all those registered with employment exchanges were literate migrants from the rural areas (Census, 1981). A large majority of such migrants, particularly the semi-literate or illiterates, were forced into the informal small sector of low-wage activity (Mishra, 1987). The population engaged in the organized sector has also been increasing steadily. Under the impact of education, social change, and rising aspirations, the profile of such working people has also been changing (Mehta, 1978).

One of the indications of this changing profile was seen in the growing feeling of dissatisfaction among the younger people at work. Studies indicate that older employees and workers, including the managerial and supervisory personnel, showed greater satisfaction with work and life than the younger ones. Objectively speaking, the older employees would have greater family responsibilities and, therefore, they would be in need of greater income. Therefore, there is bound to be general dissatisfaction due to the rising cost of living and inadequate incomes. Interestingly, however, the younger employees showed such dissatisfaction more prominently than the older employees and workers. One of the reasons for this difference could be the rising aspirations among the youth. Compared to aspirations and expectations, their salary was meagre, status inadequate, work unchallenging and working conditions unattractive. As a result, there was much greater sense of discontent – in life and at work – among them (Mehta, 1978a, 1989a, 1993).

While the workforce was more educated than what it was some years ago, their sense of dissatisfaction was not a function of education alone. Lowly educated and uneducated young workers also showed a similar discontent with their living and working conditions. Despite their low or lack of education, the same social forces boosted aspirations among them too. The general economic and social well-being lagged far behind their expectations. At the same time, the increasing gap between the affluent and the working people created a sense of relative deprivation in the youth. This, in turn, further enhanced their sense of resentment and dissatisfaction at work and in life. In this respect, their subjective conditions mirrored their objective conditions of life (Mehta, 1978, 1994).

3.3. The Youth Unrest

Under such circumstances, it was not surprising that there was a sharp rise in the youth unrest in the country during the 1970s. According to official information, there were 7,520 instances involving strikes, etc., in 1977. This was much higher than that in the previous years. Of these instances, as many as 1,146 were violent. Till August, 1978, there were 5,838 instances of campus unrest of which 1,050 were violent. The trend was more pronounced in Bihar, Uttar Pradesh and Maharashtra. Another disturbing factor was the fact that there were only 15 per cent violent instances in the full year of 1977, while it was already 18 per cent by August, 1978. A large number of incidents could have been caused by non-academic reasons (Ross, 1969). Such a situation was radically different from that found some years ago in which 71 out of 97 student demonstrations studied were found to have been caused by educational problems.

During the decade of 1970s, there was increasing evidence of growing politicization of student protest and unrest (Mehta, 1981).

Boredum and Student Unrest

However, several studies also suggested that a sense of boredum was an important factor in student unrest. Students took to demonstrations and agitations because there was nothing better to do. There was almost a total lack of meaningful recreation and leisure-time activities in the rural areas and, to a great extent, also in the urban areas and that the most frequent pastime was just idling away time or gossiping. The system of education created a sense of boredum, which was further supplemented by lack of meaningful cultural and recreational activities (Mehta, 1979, 1978a). Under such conditions, they young people took to agitations and such other activities just for fun.

The growing volume of student unrest, increasing violence, boredum, fun-value of agitations and demonstrations, politicization of protest behaviour, increasing unemployment and worklessness, increasing volume of urban problems with ever rising cost of living and several other similar factors seemed to create an explosive situation fraught with deep implications for a socio-economic change. Would the youth unrest continue to remain a dysfunctional phenomenon, getting attached to small issues or non-issues just for fun? Alternatively, would it become a meaningful phenomenon and powerful factor in changing education and the society as a whole?

3.4. Young Rural Workers

Taking income at Rs. 40 at 1972-73 prices, 30 per cent of the total population were below this income line during the 1970s. Some other estimates put the total number below the base-line at 300 million during this period. The average per capita income in 1975 was Rs. 2.50 per day. This worked out at less than Rs. 2 per day for more than 75 per cent of our rural population. (Ministry of Finance, 1975). Such conditions persisted despite legally fixed higher minimum wage rates for employment. During this period at one of the rural education camps in the Banswara District of Rajasthan (see Chapter 5), one of the participants, Udai Singh, 20 years – a Harijan landless agricultural labourer – drew a profile of their destitution as follows :

> "Harijan families generally have many children and no land. A few of them may have one to two acres of land but without irrigation and other facilities. They earn about 3 rupees a day and have to spend much more than this. They get one day's work after waiting and sitting at home for two days. Children go to school without proper clothing and the teachers throw them out from the classes. There are boys with education up to class X but no work. We have neither bamboo nor wood for our huts. One bamboo costs Rs. 8 and we may be able to make 3 baskets from one bamboo. It is, therefore, not at all paying. Nobody listens to us, neither the Minister nor the Sarpanch nor the Patwari."

One of the dire consequences of such poverty conditions was increasing indebtedness. In Bihar, for instance, 75 per cent of the households were driven to take loans for consumption at varying rates of interest, ranging from 25 to 30 per cent, sometimes rising as high as 80 per cent or higher (Das, 1976). No wonder, Bihar is one important State where youth unrest was increasingly becoming violent.

Development Strategy

The development strategy has not benefited those sections of people who needed development the most. Despite development projects, the poor have become poorer and the rich have become richer. After several years of planned development, there were 20.5 million unemployed persons – 16.5 million in the rural areas and 4 million in the urban areas during the 1970s (Raj Krishna, 1978). As for inequality, the poorest 10 per cent of rural households owned only 0.1 per cent and the richest 10 per cent more than half of the total rural assets in 1971-72 as well as in 1961-62. In the urban areas, the assets of the top business houses increased from Rs. 250 crores to Rs. 450 crores between 1969-75. The development process in India has, therefore, been associated with increasing unemployment, poverty and inequality (*ibid*).

Education and Organization of Rural Workers

It was, then, realized (Planning Commission, 1978) that the gap between the rich and the poor could be bridged only by education and active organization of the rural poor themselves. They have to become aware not only of their socio-economic rights but also of their united power in order to achieve a better life. Despite laws for minimum wages and abolition of bonded labour and such other protective laws, such illegal and patently unjust practices have continued unabated. Therefore, the people themselves need to take initiative to secure their entitlements of work, wages, commodities and a minimum level of quality of life. The rural youth could play an important role in organizing the people for collective action in this regard.

3.5. Themes in the Imagination of Rural Youth

The planners, academicians, trade unions and political parties might talk about the need for organizing the rural poor. Such "talk" or "planning" was of no avail unless the people themselves felt concerned about it. What is the content of their thoughts and imagination in this regard? Have they been changing at the thought level? This got checked during a series of education camps for rural youth, mostly landless agricultural labour, conducted during the 1970s. Efforts were then made to understand the changing consciousness among them. While it was not possible to generalize from such limited data, the stories written by the rural youth in response to designed pictures revealed interesting pointers (see Chapter 6 for some details). Some hypotheses like the following were developed on the basis of such samples of their thought and imagination.

Vicious Circle of Poverty and Crime : Need for Employment Generation and New Skills

There was a growing sense of awareness among the rural youth—somewhat literate and educated—about the relationship between crime and destitution. They also perceived the role of money power in purchasing the protection of the establishment. This was shown in the stories written to a picture showing a policeman and two ordinary villages. A typical story read as follows :

> "As father and mother have gone, he is not getting any majdoori (work). Then children starved. The some man indulged in theft and police arrest and take them away. Nobody can get him released because he has no money and he has a second wife in his house. They also learn to steal."

An interesting aspect of the new awareness was the desire for learning new skills and for generating newer employment through industry. Such a desire was revealed in story after story written to a picture showing a work theme (a machine and some people working on it). They also revealed an interesting emerging aspiration for new skills in rural youth. Thus :

> "In this picture, people are working on some machine. In our place, we have a grinding machine, and I also want to learn such work. I have to learn weaving and motor-car repair. I will learn these."

The desire to learn new skills and the perceived need for work and new opportunities were indicative of their changing aspirations. The imagination, like the above, for newer skills was noteworthy in the rural youth who were not likely to have been exposed to urban work situation. Thus :

> "In this picture two to four persons are running a machine and it seems they are working on preparing some tools and repairing some instruments. They are getting ready to do industry work. This is good for us because in such occupation our people will get employment."

Such stories showed a desire to get involved in work and to do a good job. They also showed some kind of commitment to work and a desire to overcome bad habits and laziness. Combined with their aspiration for new skills and desire for industrial work, such an element in their thoughts was very significant.

Perceived Need for Organization

Besides the need to learn new vocational skills and their dream for newer job opportunities, the rural youth revealed an action orientation. They thought about organization and unity among themselves. Thus :

> "We are five or twenty-five persons. With all united in one organization only our future work can be completed. We understand this ourselves that we and you will live unitedly. Then our future work can be completed."

This came out more stoutly in another story :

> "This is whatever tribals and Harijans are, then it is essential that we live in unity and go in one organization and labour in the hardest possible way to work better, in better jobs and occupations. As Mahatma Gandhi taught us, we should be away from untouchability and discrimination. In this way it is essential that all of us work in unity."

What to Do Now?

A sample of thoughts and imagination, such as the above, collected from stories written in response to a set of pictures during the latter part of the 1970s indicated some evidence of their changing consciousness. This was probably more true of somewhat educated and leading youth among them. Such thoughts went beyond a sense of resentment against the authority and grievance level. They seemed to show elements of activism and initiative. They seemed to say, "We are ready to participate in programmes for socio-economic changes." Not that they were clear about such a course of action; they were confused as revealed by the following predicaments :

> "Here is a poor peasant sitting on a cot, on one side his son is sitting. He is thinking about his school fees and other expenses. Thinking what to do now. Due to poverty he cannot study further. All are thinking only what to do now. There are many who have finished education, but have no jobs. What to do now? We are only thinking this that we should get free facilities from the Government."

What to do now? They aspire for a better life, want to acquire new skills, yearn for greater job opportunities, expect benefits and entitlements from development and from government and want to work and succeed at work. They also need action, organization and unity on their part. But the big question mark remains.in their mind, What to do now? How to face the situation? How to confront their growing poverty and hardship? From where to get new jobs? How and who would create new jobs? And, above all, how to organize. Such questions are very important in themselves. They could spur strong motivation for collective action for education, organization, struggle and development.

3.6. Some Suggested Emerging Characteristics of Young Workers

The socio-economic situation like the above and the changing imagination and consciousness among both the rural and urban youth were likely to reflect in behavioural profile of the young work-force. More and more educated youth from comparatively wider social strata were entering industries like banking, insurance, stell, engineering, oil and oil refining. Along with the blue-collar, the character of white-collar workforce was also changing (Mehta, 1978a). Changes were also sweeping the minds of young rural workers including agricultural workers and other categories of rural poor, as mentioned above. However, there were significant indications to suggest that the young rural workforce was getting more and more influenced by the growing socio- economic and political reality in the country. Such psychological changes were succinctly revealed in later studies (Mehta, 1983, 1989a, 1990). Some such characteristics of young workers, particularly the somewhat educated rural and/or migrant youth, are briefly discussed below. Details can be seen elsewhere (Mehta, 1990).

Increasing Sense of Normlessness

Studies tended to indicate an increasing sense of normlessness particularly with regard to the regime and government functioning as well as functioning of work organization (Nandy, 1975; Mehta, 1976d; Kothari, 1967; Mehta, 1975). As mentioned above, young workers manifested much greater work-related dissatisfaction than the older workers (Mehta, 1994). These could be due to the rising aspiration about work and life in general. They expected more and a better quality of life. Populist appeals released by political parties and the government tended to enhance general expectations. The increasing gap between expectation and actual achievement further aggravated their sense of deprivation, dissatisfaction and resentment. This created a sense of normlessness in them. They also expected political parties and governments to be fair, equitable and to function democratically for the benefit of the people. Such expectations were not being fulfilled resulting in frustration, cynicism and a sense of normalessness, particularly among the youth. This could be described as positive anger which sought better performance from the regime in accordance with certain norms and values.

Increasing Awareness about Performance

There were definite indications of an increasing concern among the younger workforce for better performance of the political system as revealed by studies conducted during the 1960s and 1970s (Kothari, 1967; Mehta, 1976a; Mehta, 1981). They showed a tendency to question the performance of the government was indicated by the results of the 1967 elections and more dramatically by 1977, 1980 as well as 1989 general elections. They appeared willing to reprimand the ruling parties for the perceived inadequacy in their public performance. As mentioned above, the youth also tended to question the performance of management/ senior officers in their work organizations. Such increasing concern and tendency of critical questioning among the youth, particularly the rural youth, was a phenomenon of utmost importance.

Increasing Desire for Social Change

Another important emerging characteristic (Mehta, 1977a, 1979a, 1981, 1994) was articulation of a need for community/social achievement among the younger blue-collar workforce, particularly among the younger trade union leaders and leading rural youth. They tended to think more about social achievement goals like improvement in general living conditions, better working conditions, better work opportunities, better education, better performance of the public system like agriculture, health, water and banking and state enterprises. They also showed a tendency for collective action, greater social awareness and a greater sense of vigilance.

These findings indicated an emerging need for social achievement and collective assertion among the youthful workers irrespective of their education level. Seen in the context of a growing sense of normlessness, growing demand for better political and governmental performance, need for social achievement and for collective assertion among young workers was a very significant pointer for future youth activism. Such motivated and somewhat educated rural youth could become active participants and leaders of mass movements for educational and social-political and economic changes.

4

DEVELOPMENT NEEDS OF RURAL WOMEN: A Case Study of Two Tribal Districts

4.1. The Survey

THE survey was confined only to one district each of Bihar and Orissa. The selection of the districts was, therefore, important. Detailed discussions were held with the officials concerned at Patna and Bhubaneswar. These highlighted the need for going to a district where (i) no or very little vocational training facilities for women existed; (ii) rural women not only needed but already exhibited a tendency to seek gainful employment; (iii) socio-economic conditions were difficult and vocational training would have the possibility of making a difference; (iv) resource potential existed which could be utilized for creating wage and self-employment; and (v) where there were good possibilities for utilizating the trained rural women. Keeping in mind such criteria, District Santhal Parganas in Bihar and District Sundargarh in Orissa were finally selected for the survey.

Data were collected concurrently from rural/tribal women themselves about their needs and aspirations with regard to training and work; knowledgeable officials and others/such as village workers, forest officers, knowledgeable and experienced individuals, social workers and women activists in the district; and from relevant documents and reports. Interviews were conducted in local dialects, Hindi and Orriya. All the datas were obtained during August-October, 1980.

Field Work

There are six sub-divisions – Dumka, Jamtara, Sahebganj, Pakur, Deoghar, and Gooda – in the Santhal Parganas district of Bihar. It was decided to select three villages each in these six sub-divisions. The field work was conducted by four local women investigators who knew the local dialects. They followed a schedule of visits to the selected villages, interviewing preferably head women approximately 38 of households in each village. The staff researcher conducted discussions and interviews with village-level workers, social workers and officials and collected documents and information about the infrastructure, local resources and existing training facilities. Thus, they collected data from 618 women, 47 officials and other relevant sources available. In about four weeks of field work. As was expected, the Survey generated considerable interest among both local people and officials.

The Sundargarh District of Orissa has three sub-divisions. Six villages were selected in each of the sub-divisions to make a total of 18 villages for the Survey. Five local field workers, four females and a male, assisted the staff researcher in conducting the field work in the district. They worked in two teams and divided the work accordingly. Thus, they interviewed some 638 women, 70 officials, including Block Development Officers, village-level workers, villagers and other knowledgeable persons in various blocks of the district. Here also the Survey generated considerable interest among the officials, social workers and people themselves. Despite tension due to certain events in the adjoining districts, the Survey was completed as per the design.

4.2. Santhal Parganas (Bihar)

Natural Resources and Occupations

The district of Santhal Parganas in Bihar forms the south-eastern portion of the Bhagalpur Division. According to the 1971 census, the total population of the district was 3,186,908 of which 94 per cent lived in rural areas. The district extended to an area of over 5,470 sq. miles with Dumka or Naya Dumka as its administrative headquarters.

Mineral Resources

The district is not very rich in minerals. However, some important minerals are found in the district. For example, benetonite which has a special property for colour absorption; china clay, used in paper, rubber, paint and textile industry, etc., fire-clay, used for fire bricks, and small coal deposits.

Forest Resources

The district is quite rich in forest resources. Sal forms 90 per cent of the crop and is generally restricted to the lower slopes of the hills in the district. Bamboo and various other forest products are now displacing sal on the higher slopes. In addition to sal, *sabai* grass is grown on the Rajmahal hill ranges. It is used in paper industry as well as for rope-making, and is the mainstay of the economic life of the Paharias—a poorer tribal community. The sabai industry is protected by the Government. There are also plants like mahua, jackfruit, imli, siris, palas eucalyptus and neem. These and similar other plants are scattered in the district and are used for medicinal purposes.

Fisheries

The fish trade of Rajmahal and Sahibganj is known for their large turnover. Thousands of maunds of fish were transported annually from these places to Calcutta. Despite this, there was very little fishery development in the district. There was a big Government owned trade centre, Gangapath Islampur Fishery Estate, on the two high banks of the Ganga. Some displaced fishermen from East Pakistan (now Bangladesh) are rehabilitated here. They are experts in fishing. There was a large untapped potential for development of fisheries in the district.

Occupations and Women

As per the 1971 Census, of the total population of 3,186,908 persons, 36.69 per cent or 1,169,310 persons, as seen in Table 4.1 constituted its workforce. Of this 60.48 per cent were cultivators and 25.38 per cent agricultural labourers. This was true for both men and women. In other occupations, there was a very clear gender bias in favour of men. For instance, against every three men engaged in mining, forestry, fishing, plantation and allied activities, there was only one woman. There were few women workers in manufacturing other than household industry. The same was true for commerce and trade. Most women workers were thus, besides agriculture, employed in home-based industry.

TABLE 4.1 : Workforce and Occupations in Santhal Parganas : 1971

	Occupation	Male	Female
1.	Cultivators	551652	481787
2.	Agricultural Labourers	66427	57969
3.	In mining, quarrying, livestock, forestry, fishing hunting and plantation, ochards and allied services	39659	12159
4.	In Household Industry	41373	26786
5.	In Manufacturing other than Household Industry	10535	1304
6.	In Construction	2400	69
7.	In Trade and Commerce	22171	3020
8.	Transport and Storage	11535	62
10.	In Other Services	60325	14035

Source : 1971 Census.

4.3. Industry and Training in the District

Sericulture

Discussions with district officials and relevant documents revealed that some 11,000 persons were engaged in rearing tusser silkworms. There was a proposal, during 1979-80, to introduce mulbery plantation in Rajmahal, Barhet, Borio, Kathikund, Amarpara and Saryahat areas of the district and to initiate yarn-making and weaving in these areas.

Poultry Farming

Poultry farming has been an important subsidiary occupation of the tribals in the district. There was a Poultry Development Centre at Dumka and four Extension Centres—one each at Jamtara, Nala, Maheshpur and Hiranpur. There were also six Poultry Hatching Centres—one each at Boarijore, Jama, Mahespur, Taljhari, Raneshwar and Sarath. Poultry farming had considerable potential for development in the district.

Lac Industry

Lac or shellac has been an important flourishing industry in the district. This is an old-time industry which has seen ups and downs. For instance, there were 12 registered factories in 1952 employing nearly 850 workers. In later years, these factories shut down one by one. Pakur was once the hub of this industry. Slowly, it lost it all. All this happened only during three years ending 1958-59. The principal cause of this downfall was probably the slump in the foreign market. There was also a practice of unlimited speculation coupled with underquoting which resulted in a constant fluctuation in the day-do-day prices. There was also very little demand of lac within the country. Attempts were needed to create an internal market and to revive the lac industry in this district.

Handloom and Powerloom Industry

There was a proposal to boost handloom and powerloom industry by providing bank loans at 4 per cent interest; improved looms on 50 per cent subsidy and 50 per cent loan basis; one-month-long training for weavers on stipend basis and workshop sheds to needy weavers. There was a need for common facilities for dyeing, printing and calendering as well as sizing of beams. It was also proposed to conduct a entrepreneurship development programme to motivate small business at the local level.

Other Industries Planned

The district administration had planned to launch 16 agro-based industries with 113 units; 16 forest-based industries with 74 units; 10 mineral-based industries with 15 units; 5 livestock industries with 7 units and 3 textile-based industries with 13 units in the year 1979-80. In addition to these, 55 demand-based industries with 88 units were also proposed. It was estimated that such 310 units in 106 types of industries, with a total investment outlay of Rs. 148.34 lakhs, would provide employment to 3,699 persons. It was further proposed to establish some 30 cottage industries in the tribal areas with a total investment of Rs. 90 lakhs providing employment opportunities to 130 persons.

Existing Training Facilities

Occupational/vocational training has been traditionally only for educated persons. This was true for both pre-service and on-plant training. Thus, in 1972, out of 207 in-service courses offered in the State (Ministry of Labour, 1972), barring just eight, entrance qualifications for all required eight years of schooling or above. There was not a single course for illiterate persons – urban and rural. The eight courses offered were in blacksmith, leather work, cutting and tailoring, embroidery and classical dances and required some education for admission. There were 92 on-plant courses all of which required an entrance qualifications of schooling up to class VIII along with some prior technical training from institutions like the Industrial Training Institute (ITI). Each of such entrance qualifications denied access to such training facilities to the vast majority of people – the illiterate men and women, in both urban and rural areas – more so in rural and remote tribal areas.

Industries Specifically for Women

The officials also revealed plans for launching of some specific industry and training for women in vocations like *dona* and *patal* (cup and plate) making from sal leaves; *papad* (a kind of snack) making; pickles, rope-making; tusser spining and reeling; tusser-weaving; soap-making, etc. There were two sericulture institutes in the district, one at Nathnagar (Bhagalpur) and the other at Chaibassa. The former had been in existence for a long time. The new one at Chaibassa was supposed to cater to the needs of tribals including women. The minimum qualification required for admission was, however, matriculation.

Thus, the district was known for its rich natural resources – minerals, forests, fisheries and lac. Three-fourths of its workforce was, however, engaged in agriculture either on their own land, and/or as tenants and/or as agricultural workers. Despite good natural resources, there were not many industries. The proportion of women gainfully engaged in non-agricultural work was very low. Most of thus engaged were employed in some home-based industry. Training facilities were, on the whole, very inadequate and for rural women these were almost nil. Whatever facilities existed were almost exclusively for literate and educated persons leaving the vast majority without access to any kind of human resource development. As could be expected, the rural/tribal women were doubly hit by such an unequal situation. The present study was conducted in this background.

4.4 Needs and Interests of Rural Women in Santhal Parganas

Social Background

The social background of the interviewed women varied from sub-division to sub-division. For instance, 85 per cent of them in Sahebganj sub-division and 45 per cent in Godda sub-division were tribals whereas people in Deogarh sub-division were almost all non-tribals. Here, some 40 per cent of them came from the scheduled castes and the rest from the backward communities. On the whole, 612 women were interviewed from six sub-divisions of the district of whom 58 per cent came from the scheduled tribes, 12 per cent from the scheduled castes and the remaining from other sections.

Interestingly, more than 70 per cent of the women interviewed were living in nuclear families. Most of them were young – 10 per cent below 20 years of age, 40 per cent between 21 and 30 years and 35 per cent between 31 and 40 years of age. Most of these women nearly 86 per cent – were illiterate. One-tenth of them had no children, 38 per cent had 2, 34 per cent 3 to 4 and the rest more than 4 children. It was noteworthy that most of the women lived not only in nuclear families but also enjoyed small to medium family size.

Income Status

As was expected, 66 per cent of the interviewed women had no income and the remaining one-third earned less Rs. 100 to Rs. 200 per month. Thus, some 76 per cent worked outside their homes. As mentioned above, a large number of women were working either as cultivators and/or agricultural labour. This was confirmed by the number of working women, 90 per cent of whom were reported to be engaged in some unskilled work. The data confirmed the fact that the poorer the women, the harder the physical work they put in.

Income Not Sufficient

The women's (and also men's) hard work did not help then much. Although, men and women both worked, only 8 per cent of the women reported that their household income was sufficient. The picture was more or less the same in all the sub-divisions, except Dumka, where practically every household was short of income. Most of them were forced to borrow and get in-debted to moneylenders. Some of them were driven to begging. Thus, the large majority of them lived in abject poverty.

Choice of Skills

It was interesting that, in this context of hard unending labour, women, by and large, appreciated the importance of vocational skills in generating income. Some of them possessed some skills such as bamboo-making, mat-making and sewing. Two-thirds of the women interviewed showed enthusiasm about learning new skills. Understandably, 90 per cent of such women wanted to learn sewing, 58 per cent wished to learn knitting, 40 per cent wanted to learn the use of spining and wheel and some 24 per cent wanted to learn lace-making. Further, some 97 per cent of them hoped that their income would go up after learning such skills. It was notworthy that such a large number of illiterate and remotely located tribal women showed vocational awareness. It also showed their keen desire to improve their purchasing power and quality of life.

Perceived Constraints and Inhibiting Factors in Learning New Skills

Though they wished to learn new skills, they considered their poverty as the most important inhibiting factor. Very few of them perceived lack of time as an inhibiting factor. In fact, three-fourths of them perceived that there was no inhibiting factor at all except money, indicating some degree for sense of efficacy in this regard. They did no show any sense of helplessness or a sense of incapability. Instead, they recalled economic factors as the cause of their problems.

4.5. Sundargarh District (Orissa) : Existing Employment and Potential

The district of Sundargarh is bounded in the north by Ranchi district of Bihar, on the west and north-west by Raigarh district of Madhya Pradesh, on the south and south-east respectively by Sambalpur and Dhenkanal districts and on the east by Sighbum district of Bihar and the Keonjhar district. The district, as it was, did not form a compact geographical unit and is extremely irregular in shape. It extended over an area of 9,675 sq. kms. It had a population of 1,030,758 persons (530,836 males and 499,922 females) in 1971. With three sub-divisions and 19 police stations, it ranked tenth in area and eleventh in population among the districts of Orissa. However, in terms of population, it was one-third of the size of Santhal Parganas. There was a phenomenal growth in population of Panposh sub-division, due to the steel industry at Rourkela. Out of three sub-divisions, Sundergarh proper was the most thickly populated area having 42.85 per cent of the population and Baine was the smallest sub-division of the district.

Traditional Crafts and Cottage Industry

Historically and traditionally, Sundergarh district comprising the two former princely states of Gangpur and Bonai, has been famous for gold-washing and iron-smelting. The men and women of the Jhora caste were known for their skill in gold-washing. This occupation is now almost defunct. Bonia has also been famous for tusser cocoons. In fact, they were exporting this silkworm in the beginning of the 20the century. However, artificial cultivation of tusser worms did not flourish as the local people considered this as an impure occupation. Tusser cocoons and stick lac were the most valuable of the forest products. Prior to independence, Birmitrapur was the only place in the State with limestone mining. The establishment of cement factory at Rajganjpur in 1951 and the steel plant at Rourkela in 1955 stimulated industrial development in the district. The district was the most industrially advanced one in Orissa where some 17.29 per cent of the total working population, as per the 1971 Census, was engaged in industrial activities, including mining and quarrying. Besides iron ore and limestone, manganese, dolomite and fire-clay are also found in the district. Major industries in the district included steel plants, fertilizers and chemicals, cement, machinery, detonators, and explosives, manufacture of refractories, etc.

Besides big industries, there were also some small industries in the district. In 1972, some 322 small factories employed 2,240 workers. There were also some food-processing units including rice and oil mills, flour, ice and ice-cream units etc. Such 57 units employed 364 workers. There were some mills, chemical, electric and such other units which employed another 200 workers during 1971-72.

Cooperatives

The State Government had taken some steps to promote cooperative movement among the weavers, artisans and others. Thus, during 1966-67, there were 26 weaver societies having 1,903 members with 11,863 looms and 374 artisan cooperatives in the district. The situation improved only slightly over the next few years. Such societies could generate only few jobs.

Some new artisan cooperatives were registered during 1979-80 and 1980-81 enrolling 267 members. Some of the trades were recognized by the Khadi and Village Industries Board and the Integrated Tribal Development Agency for assistance in the purchase of raw materials, etc. There was also one tribal women cooperative society which helped in manufacturing of shinguard used as safety equipment in mines and quarries. In addition to the fact that the cooperative movement was generally weak, it was almost fully dominated by males.

Occupations

Table 4.2 gives an idea of the occupational classification of the working people in the district as revealed by the 1971 Census. About one-third of the total population was in the categories of workers with 293,053 male and 31,069 female workers. Mostly, people were engaged in agriculture and related activities. More women worked as agricultural labourers than as cultivators. They were also employed as manual workers in mines. Interestingly, a large number of persons worked in the organized sector. Women also got employed in modern plants. This probably gave a distinct occupational character to the district. Another noteworthy fact was that, besides the organized industry, the informal sector of forestry, livestock, fishery and such allied occupations also continued to be male-dominated.

Some Specific Artisan Projects

The district authorities reportedly floated some 824 artisan projects during 1980-81. These included bidi-making, wood articles, carpentry, cane and bamboo work, food preservation, leather polishing, etc. Women were also involved in some of these projects particularly in bidi-making, food preservation, oil extraction, cane and bamboo work, handloom, khadi and tailoring.

TABLE 4.2 : Workers in Sundargarh District

Category	Male	Female
Cultivators	1,34120	5907
Agricultural Labourers	46281	8016
Forestry, Livestock Fishery and allied activities	4731	996
Minies, Quarries	8317	4252
Household Industry	7063	1791
Manufacturing in Organized Industry and Service	92541	10107

Source : 1971 Census.

4.6. Training Facilities – Not for Women

There were meagre training facilities, and most of them were meant only for the educated males. For example, in 1972 (Ministry of Labour, 1972a), there were some 86 institutional training courses in the whole State, which admitted persons with minimum school education up to class VII. The DIC conducted some entrepreneurship development and artisan training courses during the 1978-81 period, which were again mostly for males. Thus 50 artisans were trained in 1978-79, 176 during 1979-80 and 1,032 during 1980-81 in the district. Some entrepreneurship courses were also organized in 1979-80 for women, who were then expected to take up self-employment in trades like rope-making, pottery, etc.

Thus, despite industrial development, women employment and training functions were largely neglected in the district. The existing facilities were mostly for school-educated males. No attention was paid to the needs of illiterate people, particularly rural women. Although the district was minerally rich with a long tradition of skilful crafts, the rural people were hardly benefited by such resources.

4.7. Needs and Interests of Rural Women

The Survey

As mentioned above, some 638 rural women were interviewed in the Sundergarh district. Nearly half of the sample consisted of tribal women, one-tenth came from the scheduled castes and the rest from other communities. The proportion of tribal women was nearly 66 per cent in Panposh and only 38 per cent in Bonai sub-division. It was interesting to find that nearly three out of four women interviewed lived in nuclear families. More than half of the sample reported having two to four children in their families. Only 18 per cent reported having more than four children. On the whole, therefore, women in the sample survey were not only living in nuclear families but also enjoyed a small-to-medium family size.

Most of the women included in the sample were young, between 21-40 years in age. Nearly 8 out of every 10 of them were illiterate. Only 3 per cent of them had sufficient education. Most women, however, showed some knowledge of accounting, measurements and weights. Most of them had no personal income of their own. Some of them earned only about Rs. 100 a month. Although there was some variation in the reported total household income across the sub-divisions of the district, nearly 40 per cent of the total sample reported to have to stable income and another 28 per cent got income up to Rs. 200 per cent. The data suggested that, on the whole, at least 40 per cent of the sampled women belonged to households subsisting below or around the poverty line.

About 80 per cent of the women reported to have sufficient free time at their disposal. Interestingly, 92 per cent of the women from Bonai sub-division reported to have free time and also the least income in the district. Most of the women idled away their time in gossiping and just doing nothing. However, one-half of them reported to be engaged in some very low income generating activity. They had practically no hobbies excepting that some of them talked of sewing and knitting.

Most women did not go out of their homes and neighbourhood. Only one in every five women was away from homes daily for five hours or more. But the tendency to work outside the home was substantially more among the women in Panposh sub-division of the district where some large industries were located.

Nature of Work and Skills

Of the women working outside home, a large majority, more than 80 per cent, learnt their skill or trade or work, if at all it required any learning, at home or in the neighbourhood. Only a very small number had got training in some institution. Their work was, however, mostly routine manual activity which two in every three women disliked. This was also irregular and there was no continuity and stability in their work. Nearly 30 per cent of them were helping their husbands in their various occupations, doing odd manual jobs.

Women's Awareness about Training

Unlike women in Santhal Parganas, about 9 out of every 10 women in the sample showed no awareness of skill which could help them generate income. On probing, two-thirds of them expressed preference for learning sewing and such other home-based skills like knitting. Many of them thought they would be able to earn some money after acquiring such skills. Interestingly, therefore, although they earnestly needed to generate income, they were not aware, how and which skills could help them. Thus, the modern stell plant and related industry in the district seemed to have made no difference in the women's cognitive horizon. Its impact, if any, seemed to have bypassed them.

4.8. The Emerging Picture

In addition to interviewing women, some 47 knowledgeable persons in Santhal Parganas and 70 in Sundargarh district were also interviewed in connection with the present Survey. Such persons included district officials, teachers, social workers and some NGO officials. All of them were related, either in their official capacity or as non-government functionaries, with various development activities in the district. Such influential officials and opinion-makers provided valuable information regarding forest and mineral resources, traditional crafts and skills, employment and training opportunities, capability of the local people, their needs and problems and about on-going development activities in the district. They also suggested a broad plan for promoting training and employment of rural/tribal women in their respective districts. They emphasized the need for irrigation and water supply, small and cottage industry and food-for-work for generating employment in their areas. They also stressed the need for land reforms and development of infrastructure like electricity, transport and other such facilities to support employment generating activities.

The insights and suggestions of the officials and non-officials were integrated with the perceptions and needs of the local rural/tribal women in order to develop a comprehensive understanding of the training and employment needs of the local people. The obtained information, thus, culled out along with secondary data regarding existing training and employment facilities for women were then summarized to develop a profile of the district and the rural women in the two districts. These are briefly described below. Following such a profile, the training needs of rural/tribal women and a suggested action plan in this connection are discussed in Section 11.

4.9. Sundargarh District

The district is famous, historically, for its gold-washing and iron-smelting crafts and now for its large-scale industrial complexes like Rourkela Steel Plant and mines and quarrying particularly in Sadar and Panposh sub-divisions.

The Rural Women

The profile of rural women showed the following : (i) The people were marked by wide-spread poverty, with 40 per cent of the present sample living around or below poverty line. (ii) The women had sufficient time at their disposal. (iii) Most women were generally, although not meaningfully, aware of the importance of skills. Most of them had no hobbies and/or traditional skills of their own. A large number of them showed interest in sewing, knitting and such domestic skills. They hoped to be able to earn some income after learning such skills. (iv) A large majority of the women are illiterate and there was practically no opportunity for any institutional learning for women. Whatever little skills they had were learnt at home and/or in the neighbourhood. Thus, the public system of education, training and employment seemed to hve bypassed them.

Natural Resources

Several forest products and minerals were available in the district. Resources like bee-hives, mahua seeds, palm leaves, tusser cocoons, sal, kusum leaves, bamboo, fruits, lac, gum, sawai grass, medicinal herbs, charcoal, etc., provided good potential for use in training and entrepreneurship. This suggested the feasibility and importance of training in order to capitalize on such resources for generating greater employment and income for women.

Absence of Training

The District Industries Centre and the district administration were reportedly engaged in some training and development programmes. There were some small attempts by voluntary agencies also in this respect. However, interestingly, none of the women could recall to have benefited from such schemes. Also no body perceived any benefit from any institutional training programme. It was evident that whatever training facilities existed were very meagre and the people were not even aware of their existence.

4.10. Santhal Parganas

The district was rich in various forest products. There was particularly good possibility of development of fisheries. The tribals were quite familiar with poultry farming. The women, particularly the tribal women, were, traditionally, working women. For every two males engaged in the household industry, there was one female. A large number of female workers were engaged in cultivation and the number of female agricultural labourers was almost equal to the number of male agricultural labourers.

Most rural families were living below or around the poverty line. Most of the women, although illiterate, knew simple accounting and measurements. Availability of time was not a constraint for them. One in every three tribal women tried to utilize her time in some economic activity. Many of them were, however, forced to idle it away for want of work. They keenly desired to have some gainful occupation. They were even prepared to be away from home for work. Most of them, in fact, remained away for 2 to 3 hours, some for many as 7 to 8 hours, daily either for work or in search of work.

There was neither enough work opportunity nor training facility in the district. One in every three women possessed some traditional skills which they had learnt in their neighbourhood and/or at home. Training institutions hardly reached them at all. Because of their lack of education and money, the doors of the existing training courses were closed for them.

Most women helped their husbands in their occupations and were exposed to the world of work. This enabled them to see the importance of skills in increasing income. They were keen to acquire such skills. Their knowledge in this regard, however, was very limited and they could not recall skills beyond bamboo work, mat-making, sewing, etc. It was not surprising, therefore, that as many as 90 per cent of them wanted to learn only such skills particularly, sewing. The next preference was knitting, spinning and lac-making.

The district was rich in forest and mineral wealth with a good potential for several kinds of industries. The rural/tribal women themselves and the officials/social workers were aware of such resources. They saw a strong possibility of employment, entrepreneurial and vocational development in areas like basket-making, sewing, weaving, embroidery, spining, knitting, fruit preservation, durri-making, soap-making, cane furniture, livestock, etc.

4.11. Training Needs of Rural/Tribal Women

Several kinds of vocational and development needs of rural women in the districts of Santhal Parganas (Bihar) and Sundergarh (Orissa) were suggested by the Survey. Such needs were rooted in the available natural resources, traditional skills and crafts and the people's potential, and in the market for employment/selfemployment. Some suggested areas and ideas for a feasible plan of vocational development are shown in Tables 4.3 and 4.4. As there was no or very little existing training facility in the given districts, efforts had to be made almost from scratch. The survey suggested the need for priority attention to developing trades/jobs based on forestry and livestock. As is well known, minor forest products provide the greatest potential for employment/self-employment for women in our rural areas, particularly in tribal areas. In a separate study also, these emerged

TABLE 4.3 : Areas of Possible Vocational Development for Women in Sundargarh (Orissa).

Forestry	Livestock	Horticulture	Miscellaneous
1. Non-edible oilseeds and soap-making	1. Crossbreed	1. Bee-keeping	1. Tusser culture
2. Palm leave products and mat-making	2. Poultry	2. Sundrying of fruits and vegetables	2. Sericulture
3. Beedi-making	3. Piggery	3. Canning and preservation of fruits and vegetables	3. Processing of cereals and pulses
4. Collection, Classification and processing of herbal and medicinal plants.			4. Pottery
5. Production of lac and shellec			5. Pisciculture (fish ponds)
6. Making of essential oils from various seeds			6. Knitting, lace-making and embroidery
7. Rope-making			7. Weaving and durri-making
8. Golden-grass			8. Tailoring and needlework
9. Cottage match-making			9. Hand-made paper making
			10. Making of rural household material
			11. Hand-gloves making and other safety goods
			12. Toy-making

TABLE 4.4 : Areas of Possible Vocational Development for Women in Santhal Parganas (Bihar)

Forestry	Livestock	Horticulture	Miscellaneous
1. Non-edible oil	1. Crossbreed dairy goats	1. Bee-keeping	1. Tusser culture
2. Palm-leave products and mat-making	2. Poultry	2. Sundrying of fruits and vegetables	2. Sericulture
3. Beedi-making	3. Piggery	3. Canning and preservation of fruits and vegetables.	3. Processing of cereals and pulses
4. Collection, classification and processing of herbal and medicinal plants			4. Pottery
5. Production of lac and shellac			5. Pisciculture (fish ponds)
6. Making essential oils from various seeds			6. Knitting, lace-making and embroidery.
7. Rope-making			7. Weaving and durri-making
			8. Tailoring and needle-work
			9. Hand-made paper making
			10. Making of rural household materials

as priority tasks of agricultural extension for women engaged in agriculture (Mehta, 1991).

Vocational Training : Need to Expand Horizon

Women's perceptions of their needs and the suggestions given by the opinion-makers showed differences across various sub-divisions of the given district. However, sewing, knitting, weaving, lac-making and embroidery work were considered as the needs in all areas of both the districts. As could be expected, the women knew about sewing and knitting and thought that proficiency in such skills would help them earn some money. While it was necessary to provide facilities in order to satisfy such expressed needs of rural women, it was also essential to expand their horizon in order to help them understand other vocational needs and development possibilities. Vocational training has been stipulated by the National Literacy Mission (Ministry of HRD, 1988) as a means of empowerment of women. There was enough scope for such development in the districts. It was, therefore, not only a vocational but a larger social question of development. There was a need for education, cognitive development and empowerment of women to enable them to go beyond the traditional thinking in this regard.

4.12. Suggested Action Plan

Based on previous experience, infrastructural facilities available and material and social conditions of the rural households, and in view of the urgent need for providing quick employment, it would be helpful to plan for low-cost job opportunities. The survey results suggested that quick employment could be provided by reviving and upgrading traditional skills and crafts. Both women themselves and the knowledgeable local persons underlined such a need.

Diversifying Agriculture

Most working women, i.e. those working outside their homes, were engaged in some kind of cultivation work or were working as agricultural labourers. The rural women possessed certain agricultural skills which could be used for developing diversified agricultural and agro-industrial employment opportunities. In this connection, dairy, horticulture, poultry, piggery and goat-farming were suggested as viable projects for providing employment/ self-employment opportunity. Besides being labour-intensive, such projects were likely to yield much-needed nutrition for children and others in the family. Traditional skills could be further upgraded by providing appropriate training in these areas (Ministry of Rural Development, 1979). Such a need for training in agro-based crafts/industry was stressed by farmers and agricultural extension experts in a country-wide study. This was particularly important for women engaged in agriculture (Mehta, 1991). Such a view was further reinforced by tribal/rural women in eastern Uttar Pradesh, who tended to resist vocational training in stitching and knitting and desired to acquire marketable skills (Mehta, 1992).

Relevance of Training and Need for Infrastructure

Past experience of employment generating training for both men and women in the rural areas is very meagre. However, the experience of Trysem (Ministry of Rural Development, 1979a) in both the districts under review, showed that such training was not linked with local employment needs. The women were not aware of such activities and the local leaders were sceptical about its usefulness. In addition to lack of relevance, there was hardly any follow-up of such training. One major constraint in this connection was lack of appropriate infrastructure which prevented the trained artisans from utilizing their skills. The people themselves tended to think that such training hardly made any difference for them.

Image of Government and Need for Participation

The rural/tribal women themselves as well as social workers and some officials were not happy with the government handling of development programmes. They had a better image of the Central Government than the State Government. They showed preference for some kind of autonomous organisation. Although they talked of Mahila Mandals, most of them thought these were defunct. Women's aspirations and efficacy suggested a good possibility of self-initiated organization in this respect. Experience of other tribal areas showed that men and women could take initiative with some outside help in this respect. They could organize themselves for collective self-action, launch viable socio-economic projects including educational and training activities (Mehta, 1983, Chandra and Mehta, 1984). They would, however, need social skills and education in this respect also.

Provision of training facilities was no guarantee that they would be properly utilized and that people concerned would be able toderive full advantage. It was necessary to generate awareness and develop skills for organization and participation of women to enable them to take avantage of training facilities in a wider sense. There was, therefore, a need for a non- traditional people's organization for creating employment opportunities and for human resource development of women.

Innovative Organization

There was a need for innovation in this respect. A district-level autonomous society to plan, initiate and implement training may be one way of promoting participation of the women concerned. The people/women needed to be encouraged to form and register such societies/organizations with the help of voluntary organization, social workers and the women themselves. There could be further sub-divisional or block-level organization linked with the district-level organization. Such organizations could be responsible for not only training but also educational and organizational activities designed for generating employment, supply of credit, materials, equipment and marketing facilities. They may also coordinate various training and employment generating activities in the urban district/block.

A state-level organization/cooperative could coordinate the activities of similar organizations at the district level. It needs to be emphasized that participation of rural women and their self-initiated action should be central to such an organization. Considerable educational and organizational efforts are required to develop such organizations. Trade unions, educational institutions and development agencies can play an important role in this respect.

Training of Trainers/Instructors

The success of training/plans greatly depend on the availability of adequately trained and knowledgeable teachers in various crafts and skills. Organizers and trainers are required also for promoting organization and participation of rural women. Women teachers/trainers with knowledge of the local dialect are required for implementation of training and development plans. One of the earliest tasks of the proposed district/state-level organization should be to arrange for the training of teachers/instructors/trainers/organizers. Appropriate plans and syllabi, etc., would have to be prepared in this respect. What is being emphasized here is the importance of trained, preferably local, female workers for success of vocational development plan for rural women.

Need for Preparatory Work

The Survey suggested the need for some minimum preparatory work for effective training programmes. As mentioned above, there was a need to locate training in the neighbourhood with provision for an adequate stipend, trained teachers, preferably women with knowledge of local conditions and dialects. It was essential to forge linkage for training with production centres, supply of raw material and equipment, promotion of self-employment and wage employment, and with arrangements for marketing of the products. The Survey brought out the need for suitable follow-up activities along the above lines in a comprehensive way. Without such related actions, even good training was not of much avail.

As the experience suggested, most training programmes for rural people either failed or did not show the desired results because there was no appropriate follow-up after training. The trainees could not get the desired work and, therefore, they lost faith in training/development itself. It was necessary to link training with development and with employment/self-employment. Most of the training programmes should, therefore, be located at training-cum-production centres, with an appropriate infrastructure. Additionally, these training-cum-production centres should also develop facilities for marketing. It is envisaged here that women would get help in procuring materials, equipment and other facilities for carrying on their work at home.

Need for Innovative Institution Building

Thus, an autonomous type of organization at district and block level; training of teachers/instructors/organizers; attention to processes of management for effective functioning; multi-skill training-cum-production centre for each sub-division with adequate provision for appropriate mobile training facilities; innovative approach to linking training with development and employment/self-employment; appropriate provision for marketing; gradual and planned development after generating success experience at various levels; and provision for adequate stipend, equipment, materials and credit supported by the local initiative and relevant institutions may go a long way in meeting the development needs of rural women; in promoting their human resource and skill development and in generating employment/ self-employment for them.

It was clear from the Surveys and from other studies that the women needed to organize themselves in to association/societies/ unions in order to release their motivation for taking initiative for generating employment and other activities, as was done by tribal women in the Ranchi district of Bihar (Mehta, 1983). It was, therefore, necessary to help them with social skills also, for their self-employment projects. They needed skills in entrepreneurship, readiness for taking some simple and modest risk, action planning for simple projects. readiness for acting on the environment, support system and credit institutions. The income generation as well as self-employment, therefore, needed to be linked with a desire for better quality of life, readiness for collective action and for forming and working in organizations.

5

WELL-BEING OF UNORGANIZED WORKERS : The Case of Central Welfare Organization

STATUTORY funds have been created in India to provide welfare facilities with a view to improving the quality of life of unorganized and scattered workers like those in mica, iron-ore and manganese-ore mines and the beedi industry. These funds are administered by country-wide welfare organizations with several zonal offices. This chapter presents case studies of organization and management of sectoral programmes like health, water supply, housing and education. These suggest a mismatch between the structure and administrative practices and the goals of the programme. The welfare activities were also not in accordance with the national health policy. The study suggests the need for organizational changes, bureaucratic reorientation, training of personnel, and changes in the approach and content of the various welfare programmes.

5.1. The Welfare Funds

Certain categories of workers, such as those engaged in coal-mining, mica-mining, iron-ore mining, limestone-mining, etc., live and work under very difficult conditions. Many such mines and workplaces are scattered in remote areas without access to medical, water, education and other such facilities. In view of such difficult conditions, the Government of India has, from time to time, initiated legal and administrative interventions designed to specially take care of the well-being of such workers. Statutory funds have been created to provide continuing and sound financial support to such welfare programmes.

One of the earliest efforts for collecting such funds was the Mica Mines Welfare Fund Act of 1946 which was enacted for levy and collection of cess on the exported mica to promote well-being of the labour employed in the mica-mining industry. The Iron Ore Mine Labour Welfare Cess Act was enacted in 1961 which came into force with effect from October 1, 1963. This act has been amended from time to time to extend its scope and also to cover manganese ore mine workers. The Lime stone and Dolomite Mine Labour Welfare Fund Rules, 1973, came into force with effect from December 1, 1975. A very significant step was taken by the government in 1976 when it was decided to provide a special programme for the benefit of workers engaged in the beedi industry. Prior to this, the emphasis was only on mine labour. With the promulgation of the Beedi Workers' Welfare Cess Act, 1976, and the Beedi Workers' Welfare Fund Act, 1976, a new chapter was opened in the history of labour welfare movement in the country, highlighting the need for specially designed and administered programmes for various categories of unorganized and vulnerable working people.

Objectives of Welfare Programmes

The guiding principle and the ultimate aim of the various welfare programmes from the very inception has been the improvement of the standard of living of the workers concerned. Some of the important objectives of such programmes have been as follows :

1. Improvement of public health and sanitation; prevention of diseases and provision and improvement of medical facilities.
2. Provision and improvement of water supply and facilities for washing.
3. Provision and improvement of educational facilities.
4. Improvement of standard of living, including housing and nutrition, amelioration of social conditions, and provision of recreational facilities.
5. Provision of transport to and from the place of work.

Thus, the main intended thrust of the various welfare programmes was to help the concerned workers improve their quality of life through public health, sanitation, prevention of disease, access to medical facilities, provision and improvement of water supply and washing facilities, access to utilization of educational facilities and by providing housing, nutrition, recreational, transport and such other facilities. It was visualized that the various welfare funds and programmes would effectively intervene for promoting dignity and quality of life for such unorganized and neglected workers.

5.2. Welfare Organizations

In order to administer the various funds and to develop and implement various programmes, labour welfare organizations have been created in different regions of the country under the general charge of the Director General of Labour Welfare (DGLW) in the Union Ministry of Labour. Thus, the programmes were being administered in various regions by welfare commissioners stationed at Jabalpur, Bhubaneswar, Bhilwara, Bangalore, Allahabad and Panaji, and by deputy welfare commissioners at Barbil (Orissa) for iron ore, at Karma (Bihar) and at Hyderabad (Andhra Pradesh) for mica. The welfare commissioners of various regions were responsible for administering all the funds mentioned above and for implementing various programmes under the funds concerned. Each fund has, however, its own welfare organization, e.g. Mica Workers' Welfare Organization, Beedi Workers' Welfare Organization, etc. Each welfare commissioner is, therefore, responsible for several welfare organizations and simultaneously all of them were accountable to a central authority in the Ministry of Labour. Each organization was helped by a central advisory committee and state-level advisory committees in all the states concerned consisting of representative of employer, workers, etc., and the central and state governments, headed in most cases by respective Labour Ministers.

Thus, organizations have been created at all-India levels with zonal offices as instruments of implementing public policy for providing special welfare attention to some 3.2 million workers. Taking five members in each worker's family, the various organizations were responsible for catering to some 16 million people.

5.3. The Programmes on the Ground

Welfare programmes have been in force for quite some time – some like mica-mine welfare for longer periods than others like beedi workers' welfare which is of more recent origin. The programmes cover more or less all parts of the country with greater concentration in some States. These programmes are of vital importance for a large part of our working people and are, therefore, of great public significance. The present study was undertaken to assess effectiveness of the various interventions in improving living standards and quality of life of the workers concerned to find out the extent and reach of the various welfare programmes, and to identify organizational and management problems related to the functioning of various welfare activities.

Field Visits and Discussions

In view of the extensive nature of the study, quick visits were undertaken by the author to some selected welfare sites and detailed discussions were held with the officials concerned, trade union workers, employers, ordinary workers, and others. Thus, some mica mines in the Bhilwara and Karma regions, limestone and dolomite quarries in the Bangalore region, iron-ore mines in the Barbil and Goa regions, and beedi work sites in the Allahabad and Bangalore regions were visited for first-hand information about the living and working conditions there. Some central hospitals, static dispensaries, and such other medical centres were visited in the above areas and detailed discussions held with the medical and para-medical personnel. Similarly, some welfare institutions like multi-purpose institutions, small community centres and library and reading rooms were also visited and discussions held with the field workers concerned with these activities. There were field visits to housing sites and colonies, including homes of beedi workers in Allahabad and Bangalore areas. Each welfare organization also provided specially prepared detailed notes on its various activities, problems and needs. The present chapter is based on several case studies thus completed. The data and field reports were collected during 1981 and 1982.

5.4. Employment : Conditions of Work

Fluctuations in employment in the industries concerned and the quantum of production makes an interesting reading. For instance, as seen in Table 5.1 , the number of workers employed in iron-ore mines went down over the period of 15 years ending in 1980 by about 27 per cent whereas the production was more than doubled. There was also a slight fall, during the same period, in the number of manganese mine workers between 1977 and 1980. Here, the production also registered a slight fall. There was also a decline in the number of workers employed in limestone mines. During the same period, however, the production rose from 25.4 million tonnes to 28 million tonnes. On the other hand, the number of workers employed in dolomite mines increased during this period, whereas the production registered a slight fall.

TABLE 5.1 : Employment and Production Figures of Various Ores

	1965	1973	1977	1980
Employment				
Iron ore mines	59800	–	–	43900
Manganese	–	–	27830	26842
Limestone	–	52000	–	49752
Dolomite	–	4712	–	7527
Production (in million tonnes)				
Iron ore	22.06	–	–	43.42
Manganese ore	–	–	1.67	1.62
Limestone	–	25.38	–	27.96
Dolomite	–	1.37	–	1.31

Source : Ministry of Labour, Director-General of Labour Welfare, Standard Note (1980).

The mica mine industry also showed declining employment. For instance, the number of workers employed in the mica mines in Andhra Pradesh was about 3,000 in 1974 which went down to about 1,000 in 1981. During the same period the number of such workers in Bihar fell from around 6,000 to around 4,000. However, the tendency appeared to be erratic and reverse in Rajasthan where the number of workers employed in the mica mines was some 1,000 in 1974 and nearly 3,000 in 1980. Between 1974 and 1980, the number of workers thus employed registered a very significant fall. For instance only 314 workers were reported to have been employed in 1978 and 368 in 1979.

Comparable employment data in the beedi industry were not available. Nearly 3 million workers were reported to be employed in the beedi industry towards the end of 1981, mainly in the Bhubaneswar, Allahabad, Jabalpur and Bangalore regions. However, the welfare commissioners concerned, other officials and trade union leaders were all unanimous in their observation that the actual number of workers employed in this industry was much higher. This could be in the vicinity of as many as 5 million workers some of whom were employed in making unbranded beedis about which information was not readily available. There was a tendency on the part of the contractors and manufacturers to conceal information about the actual number of workers engaged by them.

Towards the end of 1981, there were about 45,000 iron-ore miners, 27,000 manganese-ore workers, 50,000 lime-stone and 7,500 dolomite workers, some 10,000 mica miners, and over 3 million beedi workers in the country. Thus, the number of beedi workers in the country was much larger than the combined strength of the mine workers being covered by the respective funds.

The reported fall in the number of workers, particularly in the mica mines and also elsewhere, probably indicated a tendency to manipulate such data so as not to show workers on their rolls beyond a stipulated period in order to avoid attraction of laws concerned. For instance, a mica miner working for more than 90 days continuously would be entitled to not only welfare benefits but also other service benefits. It was widely confirmed by the officials and others that the mica-mine owners deliberately concealed information and manipulated data in order to deny worker status to these miners. It was reported that the number of mica miners would be about 15,000 in the Marma mica mine fields alone. There were many illegal mines being operated. The owners also shifted their mining operations, thus increasing the number of miners employed in that period, as was the case in the Bhilwara region. At other times, they would close down some operations, causing unemployment. In fact, this tendency was listed as one of the most important reasons for the poor living conditions of the mica-mine workers and their families.

Further, it was interesting to note that the iron-ore mining industry registered an increase in output with decreased number of workers over a 15-year period. The same thing was notice with regard to limestone industry over a seven year period. This was due to mechanization, which enhanced production as well as profits. At the same time, it increased unemployment among the miners. Such a situation where workers increasingly lost jobs enhanced the utility of the welfare interventions. It was all the more necessary for the organizations to work with efficiency and commitment in order to protect the workers and to promote and sustain their well being. The following sectoral studies of welfare and public action and their organization and management should be viewed in the specific context of the needs of our vast population of unorganized workers employed in the sprawling informal sector.

5.5. Health Services

Hospital/Treatment Facilities

In iron-ore, manganese-ore and dolomite mines, the medical treatment facilities received the highest priority in various welfare programmes. The budget estimates and the patterns of expenditure for the year 1978-80, 1980-81 and 1981-82 were very revealing. For instance, in 1980-81, out of the total sanctioned budget of Rs. 3.9 million for iron-ore and manganese-ore workers' welfare in the Bangalore region, a sum of Rs. 14 lakhs was spent on providing medical facilities. Similarly, out of the total sanctioned budget of Rs. 15 lakhs for limestone and dolemite miners, a sum of Rs. 13 lakhs was earmarked for medical facilities.

Towards the end of 1981, four central hospitals—one each in Orissa (Jodda), Bihar (Barajamda), Karnataka (Karinganur), and at Goa were established with iron-ore and manganese-ore funds. In addition to these central hospitals, some of 16 static/mobile and static-cum-mobile dispensaries were established in various regions, along with services of nine ambulance vans. Similarly, medical facilities received priority attention in the welfare programme for limestone and dolomite mine workers. Some 22 dispensaries and medical units of different types, including Ayurvedic dispensaries, were established in various regions. Arrangements were made for reserving beds in related hospitals for the treatment of T.B. patients.

In addition to these facilities directly provided by the welfare organizations, there was a scheme for providing grant-in-aid at the rate of 50 per cent of the total expenditure to mine managements for improving their dispensary services and for purchase of certain hospital equipments like X-ray machines, etc. A similar grant-in-aid facility also existed under the iron-ore and manganese-ore funds. For instance, a grant-in-aid was provided to mine-owners for improving their dispensary facilities. A scrutiny of the names of mining organizations, which had received grants-in-aid revealed that most of them were organized industrial enterprises. These included Rourkela Steel Plant, Orissa Mineral Development Corporation, Orissa Mining Corporation, Chowgule and Company Pvt. Ltd., D.G. Bandokhar and Sons, and Dalmia International Hospet. A similar picture obtained with regard to limestone and dolomite mines where two large cement plants, with which the limestone mines were attached, got grants-in-aid for improving their dispensary facilities.

Medical Facilities for Mica Miners

Hospital and treatment facilities had also received top priority in the mica mine labour welfare programme. For instance, by the end of 1981, 9 central/regional hospitals, including T.B. hospitals, had been established in different regions. In addition to these, there were 14 ayurvedic dispensaries, 8 allopathic dispensaries, five mobile medical units, and three maternity and child welfare centres operating in these regions. The health organization provided some facilities for treatment of T.B. which was widely prevalent among the mica miners. There was a central T.B. hospital at Karma and also at Kalichedu (Andhra Pradesh) and a provision for 10 beds for T.B. patients in the central hospital at Gangpur in the Bhilwara region. Provision also existed for reserving some beds at some sanatoria in various regions.

Medical Facilities for Beedi Workers

Medical facilities received priority attention in the case of beedi workers also. Some 76 static and mobile dispensaries were functioning towards the end of 1981 in various regions. It was interesting to note that no such facilities were provided by the beedi manufacturers. Almost all the medical facilities were being financed by the Beedi Workers' Welfare Fund.

Field Observations

Visits to a few central hospitals in some regions did suggest that they were fairly well-equipped. They were doing commendable work and were fulfilling a great need for proper medical care in neglected areas. At some places, lack of para-medical staff and supportive medical staff was reported. In some cases, proposals for such staff were reported to be pending with the government for quite some time.

Discussions with the medical and welfare officials suggested that in some cases hospital facilities were not fully utilized. For instance, the Central Hospital at Karma had been, on an average, looking after some 3,500 indoor patients for several years. However, this number fell to around 3,200 in 1981. Similarly, the number of outdoor patients attended to during 1979 was around 47,000 which came down to 34,500 in 1981. These patients included some non-mining workers as well as several staff members and their dependents. The hospital had been handling maternity cases also. However, cases of deliveries at the hospital had been rather few. For instance, around 270 women were annually provided this service at the hospital during 1979-1981. The number of people taking advantage of family welfare facilities was still smaller, less than 40 per year were helped with vasectomy, and around 50 tubectomies were performed annually. Interestingly enough, instead of increasing, the number of people taking advantage of family welfare facilities tended to decrease. It was pointed out by the officers that such programmes were not popular among the miners' community.

Treatment of T.B.

The same tendency was noticed at the T.B. Hospital, Karma. The number of indoor patients came down from 567 in 1979 to 247 in 1981 and outdoor patients from 1,804 in 1979 to 1,732 in 1981. At the same time, the doctors reported that the incidence of T.B. in the mining areas was about 3 per cent as against the national average of 1.5 per cent. In addition to known T.B. patients, many more suffered from chest diseases. One of the reasons, for the declining number of patients, was the decline in the number of miners eligible for the welfare facilities, due to shifting employment status.

The officers thought that the mine-owners as well as the welfare rules were responsible for such a situation, particularly for the treatment of T.B. But in fact this service is free for everyone in the country in pursuance of the national programme for the eradication of this disease. Whether a person is a miner or not was, therefore, immaterial as far as treatment of T.B. was concerned, which in any case was to be free. However, the rules came in the way in this connection. They were apprehensive that there would be an audit objection if they treated non-miners free of cost. The doctors were strongly in favour of domiciliary treatment and public health approach for the eradication of T.B. However, they were not equipped for such a programme and the government rules, in this regard, came in their way.

Reluctant Doctors

Besides other reasons, the procedure for recruiting doctors was also responsible for vacant positions in the welfare organizations. At the time of the study, the doctors were recruited through the UPSC, for the Central Health Scheme. This procedure was very lengthy. Once a doctor was recruited, he took a long time to join and in many cases, he was reluctant to serve in remote areas. In some cases because of such recruitment rules, doctors were forced to work on a purely ad-hoc basis. They were naturally dissatisfied.

Summary of Health Situation

Field visits to hospitals and dispensaries, discussions with medical and welfare officials and trade union leaders, and an analysis of documents showed the following about the workers' health and the health facilities.

Widespread diseases like T.B., bronchitis, eczema, skin diseases, silicosis, water-borne diseases like worms and anaemic conditions among pregnant women were reported from various regions, particularly among mica miners and beedi workers. These were largely due to the poor living and working conditions of the workers. The emphasis was largely on treatment, rather than on prevention and education. As the poor conditions of life not only persisted, but sometimes worsened, a mere curative approach was not enough. With no let-up in their hardships, the workers tended to lose interest in treatment. At times, they faced the grim prospect of losing their job, and, therefore, bread, in case the employers identified them as sick.

According to the norms of the National T.B. Control and Prevention Programme, T.B. patients should be admitted to the hospital only for a short period and the rest of the treatment should be done at home under the supervision of a health visitor.

For some strange government rules and procedures, the doctors were not able to implement the domiciliary programme. Such factors saw the strange spectacle of unutilized hospital capacity with a number of indoor as well as outdoor patients falling. Yet, the scourge of T.B. continued to afflict the workers unabated.

In view of the sheer number of workers and their dependents involved, the facilities for beedi workers were far more meagre as compared to those being provided to more organized workers such as those in iron and manganese ore and limestone and dolomite mines.

5.6. Water Supply

Drinking water shortage was a chronic problem in many mining areas and also in areas where the beedi workers lived. Water supply, therefore, was an important priority area of the welfare programme. Rules allowed payment up to 75 per cent of the estimated cost or actual cost, whichever was less, to mine owners for sinking wells. The following interventions were implemented for the four groups of workers in this regard.

Mica Mining

A permanent water supply scheme was implemented for the mica miners in Lakichedu village in Andhra Pradesh. Work on another scheme, viz. Turimerla Water Supply Scheme, for which the Central Government sanctioned a sum of Rs. 76,750, was reported to be completed in all respects. The Mica Mine Labour Welfare Organization was waiting for the Government of Andhra Pradesh to hand over the scheme to them. In addition to these schemes, 26 drinking water wells had been sunk in this region. In Bihar, 74 wells at a cost of Rs. 7,40,000 had been sunk. In Rajasthan, 47 old wells had been renovated and 16 wells sunk for the benefit of these workers.

Iron-Ore and Manganese-Ore Miners' Welfare

The miners' welfare fund contributed to digging of wells and laying of pipelines in various areas. Subsidies were also given to the mine-owners towards construction of wells and water supply facilities. Out of 42 water supply schemes sanctioned, 29 had been completed. The Rajhara Township Water Supply Scheme and Bolani (Orissa) Water Supply Scheme were also completed. A scheme was sanctioned to Hindustan Steel Limited for Kaltara iron-ore mines in Orissa. Another Integrated Piped Water Supply Scheme for the mines in Baitrani Valley, Jodda, Orissa, with an estimated cost of Rs. 1,08,20,000 had also been sanctioned. The work on the project was to be started from October, 1980, and completed within two years. However, the work was yet to start by the time of the present field work in November 1981.

Limestone and Dolomite Mines

In the Bhubaneswar region, four wells were dug for the Dumri limestone quarries and three for the Bisra Limestone Company. Five more wells had been sanctioned for the same company. Several mining enterprises were sanctioned schemes for developing water supply for their workers. Three such companies in Jabalpur, one in Allahabad, three in Bangalore, and six in the Bhilwara region reportedly took advantage of this scheme. A sum of Rs. 200 was sanctioned to be paid per month as subsidy for water supply for K.C.P. Mines at Macherla in Andhra Pradesh. Some other enterprises were given grant-in-aid for construction of overhead tanks.

Beedi Workers' Welfare

No water supply scheme was introduced for the benefit of beedi workers, till the time of the present field work in November, 1981.

Comparative Water Situation

Comparatively speaking, the iron and manganese-ore and limestone and dolomite labour welfare organizations paid greater attention to catering to the water needs of their workers. However, here also, the overall expenditure on water supply over the 1979-1982 period was only 5 per cent of the total expenditure. In the mica area, only a few wells here and there had been dug, and the beedi workers were yet to receive any such facilities. It was thus clear that supply of clean drinking water received only scant attention. This further confirmed that, preventive health care facilities were neglected by the organizations. Further, more organized sectors like iron and manganese ore and limestone and dolomite mining industry got better attention. The interest of mica and beedi workers—the poorest of the lot—was grossly neglected. These were the very workers who bore the brunt of major diseases and ill-health.

5.7. Housing

Several housing schemes were formulated under the fund organizations. There was a Type I scheme which offered employees a subsidy of 75 per cent of the standard cost of Rs. 6,825 in ordinary areas and Rs. 7,925 in black cotton or swelly soil areas or the actual cost, whichever was less. Specifications included a verandah-cum-kitchen, a bad-room, a bathroom, and a latrine. Under the Type II scheme, the subsidy was the same, but the standard cost allowed was Rs. 11,325 in ordinary areas and Rs. 13,424 in black cotton and swelly soil areas. It provided for a minimum accommodation of 400 sq. ft. In both the schemes, maintenance, supply of water and electricity were the responsibility of the mine or factory management, while house ownership was vested in the fund organization. There was a build-your-own-house scheme under which if the worker owned a plot of 100 sq. yds. of land, within a radius of 8 km. from the mine, he could get a subsidy of Rs. 600 and interest-free loan of Rs. 900. A certificate was required from the management for getting the loan.

The progress in housing for the unorganized workers, as the present case study shows, has been very tardy. For instance, till the end of 1981 (the time, the case study was conducted), the mica workers (their Welfare Fund Act was enacted in, as early as 1946) had got some 374 houses under the build-your-own-house scheme and another 58 under the Type I scheme in Andhra Pradesh, 160 houses under Type I in Bihar, and 344 under build-your-own-house scheme in Rajasthan. The dolomite and limestone workers (their Welfare Fund came into force with effect from December, 1975) on the whole, got some 1,905 houses under various schemes. The iron-ore and Manganese-ore workers (their Fund came into force with from October, 1963) got a total of 11,545 houses, most of which were under the Type II scheme. Most of the remaining houses were constructed under the Type I scheme. A special scheme for economically weaker beedi workers was also then, under way. This was similar to the build-your-own-house scheme.

Under the scheme, the Government of West Bengal was sanctioned an amount of Rs. 5 lakhs during 1978-79. Similarly, a sum of Rs. 15 lakhs was sanctioned to the Government of Madhya Pradesh, and small sums to Tamil Nadu and Gujarat. The respective State Government were supposed to provide housing for economically weaker sections of beedi workers with these funds. Information regarding the progress of the scheme was not then available.

Comparative Housing Situation : Lessons of the Case Study

The iron-ore and manganese-ore workers enjoyed, as the case study showed, much better housing facilities, as compared to workers under other fund organizations. Here also, the beedi workers lagged far behind and the mica-mine workers were in a very bad shape. Looking at the total number of workers involved in iron-ore and managanese ore-mining industry, the number of houses constructed for them was also not encouraging. It was interesting to note that, on the recommendations of the Central Advisory Board of the Iron-Ore and Manganese-Ore Mines Labour Welfare, the Central Government had agreed to allocate 40 per cent of the total budget for housing and no difference was allowed to be made between the contract labour and the regular labour for welfare facilities. The situation on the ground was, however, quite different as the case study showed, and housing continued to receive scant attention. Both the governments and the managements of the respective Welfare Funds were largely unresponsive to such pressing and humane needs of the unorganized workers.

5.8. Education

Education occupied an important place in the objectives of the welfare organizations. In the beginning, some schools were started directly under the welfare funds. However, there was an emerging consensus in favour of handing over the schools to the respective State Governments. Instead, funds were to be utilized for pre-school education in order to supplement government efforts.

As is well known, school dropout was a serious problem, particularly in the rural and urban poor areas. For their benefit, the welfare organizations were called upon to help tackle this problem and to promote and sustain retention of children in schools. The scheme of scholarship was launched towards this end.

Scholarship Schemes

An analysis of the scholarship programme and discussions with officials concerned and other revealed that the number of children covered was very small as compared to the large numbers who needed this help. The amount earmarked for educational activities was very meagre – Rs. 6 lakhs in Andhra Pradesh, Rs. 10 lakhs in Bihar and Rs. 1.32 lakhs in Rajasthan for the year 1980-81. Some of this money was spent on mid-day meal. Eventually not even 100 children could get scholarship from the welfare funds in Andhra Pradesh and Bihar.

Field Observations

It was clear that there was a big gap between the need and the help provided. The position was a little better for the iron-ore and manganese-ore, limestone and dolomite mine workers. Discussions with the officials concerned and trade union leaders pointed to the following shortcomings and grievances in this regard :

1. The application form for scholarship was long and rather complicated. The children in lower primary classes found it difficult to fill it. In some regions, they insisted that all items in the given form be filled by children in their own handwriting. It was further reported that such forms were supplied in English only. Moreover, these forms were not supplied to schools directly; the children were required to obtain them from either a trade union or a panchayat. As a result, in some cases, as many as 60 per cent of the applications were rejected on technical grounds.
2. Not only the number, but the amount of scholarship also was very meagre. The school authorities concerned, and in some cases the State Government officials, were not cooperative. Schools run by the enterprises themselves were in a better position where children were guided by their teachers.
3. The beedi and mine workers' children were in a worse position. They got no guidance from any source. Most of them were not even aware of such a facility. On the whole,

the educational component in the welfare programme was very weak. It hardly made any difference for the children who continued to drop out from school unabatted.

5.9. Organization and Management

A Joint Secretary levei official, designated as Director General of Labour Welfare, headed the welfare wing in the Ministry of Labour, Government of India. He looked after all the above welfare funds and programmes. As is the organization pattern in government, the DGLW was assisted by a Deputy Secretary, two Under Secretaries, a Welfare Commissioner (HQ), some section officers, and clerical and personal staff at the headquarters. There was a Central Advisory Committee at the national level for each programme consisting of representatives of employers, workers and Central and State Governments,with corresponding State-level advisory committees in the States concerned. There were also several zonal welfare organizations with headquarters at Allahabad, Bhubaneswar, Bangalore, Bhilwara, Jabalpur and Panaji (Goa), each under the charge of a Welfare Commissioner. There were sub-zonal offices along with the medical and engineering wings. These organizations were patterned more or less like any other government organization. A brief tentative organization chart is shown in Fig. 5.1. Annexure I (at the end of the Chapter) gives the functions of the various sections of the central welfare wing. Several problems and grievances were discussed during meetings with the officials concerned. Some of these were also observed during field visits and in some official documents and reports.

Centralization of Powers

The organizations suffered from over-centralization. Financial sanction was given by the central office at New Delhi, which entailed frequent delays. There were instances when such sanction was counter-productive for welfare programmes like scholarships, etc. The Welfare Commissioners did not have the freedom to implement even approved welfare schemes. Such delays and centralization created not only administrative/managerial problems, but also promoted negative image (for the welfare organization) among the intended beneficiaries.

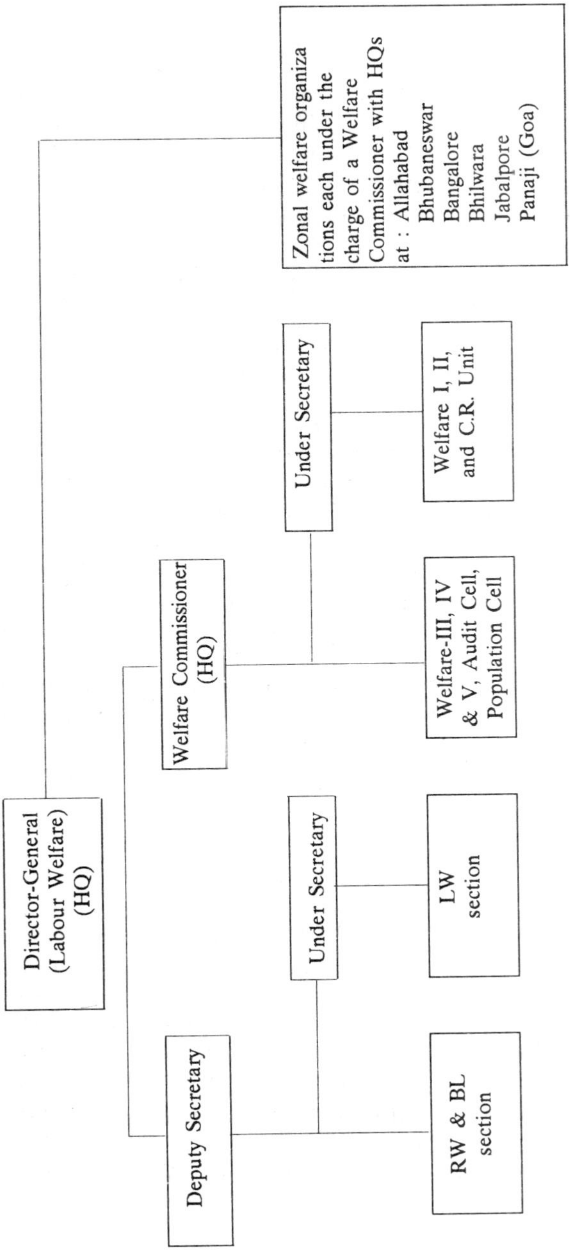

FIG. 5.1 : Organizational Chart of the Welfare Wing under the Administrative Control of Director-General (Labour Welfare)

Creditworthiness of the Organization

Each zonal organization was quite large, covering vast areas. The Welfare Commissioners alone were empowered to sign cheques for making payment. This resulted in delays which in turn lowered the creditworthiness of the organization. There were instances when diesel, servicing, repairs, etc., were not available on credit and the mobile medical units could not operate. The local dealers were not prepared to give anything on credit. Lack of delegation of such minimum powers affected the creditworthiness and efficiency of the organization.

Personnel Matters

The Welfare Commissioners and other officers were agitated about certain apparent shortcomings in personnel matters. It was pointed out that the matter relating to creation of selection grade posts for various categories of staff had been pending for a long time. The corresponding employees in other departments of the government had already been given selection grades. Such discrimination was causing deep frustration and disappointment among the employees of the welfare organizations. Approved recruitment rules were also available in some welfare organizations. For instance, there were no such rules in the Beedi Welfare Organisation. Lack of uniformity in rules caused further discontent. Those working on the same jobs were placed in different pay scales, causing immense damage to the functioning of the organization.

Lack of Promotional Avenues

Lack of uniformity in recruitment rules, qualifications criteria, and pay scales were accompanied by lack of promotional avenues for the staff in various organizations. It was repeatedly stated that, ". . . . many staff members are to retire in the same post in which they were initially appointed in service". Staff have retired after 30 years of meritorious service without getting a single promotion in their career. This was against the norms of justice. Many employees did not have anything to look forward to, no hope of any kind of promotion. Despite such a situation, the staff of the Mica Mine Labour Welfare Organisation, for example were ordered to undertake additional workload and to look after the duties and responsibilities of Beedi, Limestone and Dolomite Workers' Welfare funds in Tamil Nadu.

The Staff Strength

Most Welfare Commissioners resented the interference of the central Work Study Unit (WSU). In some cases, where the organization had been pressing hard (with the central office) for additional staff, the WSU had recommended reduction of staff. Such conflicts forced the welfare organizations to spend considerable time in voluminous paper work in order to justify sanction of additional staff. This diverted attention from welfare work and also caused insecurity among the staff. It was pointed out, for example in the Bhilwara region, that due to inadequate staff strength they were able to cover only 30 per cent of the mica-mine workers. The sanctioned housing had to be periodically inspected by competent technical authority for releasing subsidy and instalments of loans. They were not able to do so, for example, in the souther zone covering four States due to inadequate staff strength. This caused delays, hardships and hindrances in implementing welfare programmes.

Rigid Controls

As could be expected in centralized functioning, the organizations suffered from delays, avoidable paper work, and rigid, dysfunctional controls. As mentioned above, lack of delegation of powers eroded the very creditworthiness and the image of the organization. The Welfare Commissioners felt that "there cannot be a wooden approach in matters of welfare, particularly so when the whole concept of welfare was designed for weaker sections". Lack of flexibility took away initiative from the field officials. There were instances where officials who showed innovativeness and promptness found themselves in deep waters with visiting audit parties and let down by their senior officers at the central headquarters.

5.10. Some Peculiar Problems : Karma (Bihar)

Under-staffing and other personnel problems indicated lack of commitment to welfare and lack of concern for performance in the top management/administration. Such tendencies were also indicated by peculiar problems at Karma (Mica Mine Labour Welfare Organization in Bihar). It was one of the oldest welfare organizations with a well-developed infrastructure like offices, housing for the employees, hospitals, etc. The organization was, however, afflicted by certain unique ailments. These are summarized as follows : (i) Several members of the same family were working in the same office (ii) There was persistent resistance to any kind of transfer even to a place only a few miles away; (iii) There were repeated cases of thefts, pilferages (of public property, medicines, stores, etc.) and embezzlement of public funds; (iv) Employees sentenced in courts of law for criminal offenses continued to live in government quarters; (v) Departmental inquiries were ineffective as internal witnesses were forced to go hostile; (vi) Emergence of anti-social elements in the organization and their threatening postures; (vii) Emergence of vested interests among the employees who conducted business transactions with the organization itself; (viii) Last but not least, persistent tendency among certain sections of employees, such as those mentioned above, to send complaints against the officials to the central office at New Delhi. These were designed to demoralize the officers and to prevent them from taking action against the lumpen employees. There was open political interference in favour of the lumpen elements.

Increasing Expenditure and Decreasing Welfare : Karma

Karma was a unique case where the annual expenditure had been increasing with decreasing welfare programmes. Unlike all other organizations, it was reported to be overstuffed at the office level (not at the field level). The deteriorating performance was clearly due to the crippling inefficiency of the organization. On the one hand, employment for the mica-mine workers showed a sharp decline, and, on the other, illegal mining was on the increase. The net result of all this was deterioration in the quality of life of the workers.

Large Territorial Coverage

Another important problem which all organizations faced was their vast territorial coverage. For instance, the organization at

Allahabad was responsible for mica-mine labour, beedi workers, limestone and dolomite-mine workers in Uttar Pradesh, Bihar, Jammu & Kashmir and the Union Territory of Delhi. In Uttar Pradesh alone, there were some 4.05 lakh beedi workers spread over 18 districts of the State and Bihar had another 3.5 lakh beedi workers. It was reported that a team of 8 field workers was supposed to cater to the needs of some 8 lakh beedi workers scattered in many districts in many districts in two of the largest States in India. Beedi workers in Bihar were concentrated in Chakardharpur and other areas which are closer to Karma and Ranchi and the mica-mine workers are concentrated in the Karma-Kodarma area. These places are quite far from Allahabad where the headquarters of this organization was located. Sheer geographical difficulties contributed to the already complicated management problems in this region.

Lack of Welfare Attitude

It was widely reported by the welfare officials and medical officers that the attitude of most of the staff, including officials, was not welfare-oriented. Bureaucratic expansion of staff increased file work without increasing the efficiency of welfare programmes. There was no provision for any kind of training of officers and field workers.

The Hierarchies

There was a rigid hierarchy among the welfare personnel. For instance, besides the welfare commissioner, there were deputy welfare commissioner, assistant welfare commissioner, welfare administrator, assistant welfare administrator, and welfare inspectors. In addition to these, there were some field workers attached to multi-purpose institutes, etc. The pay scales of such personnel were not adequate to attract the right quality of personnel. Such hierarchical organizations tended to create rigid bureaucratic office orientation in the staff. In a way, the proliferating hierarchical structure in the welfare organizations was a replication of a similar structure in the central administrative ministry.

5.11. Security and Welfare of Unorganized Workers : Need for Integrated Strategy and Organization

Launching of welfare funds and organizations was a pioneering public intervention for the benefit of some of the neglected and unorganized sections of our workforce. These were designed to reach out to some sections of miners and beedi workers in the remote parts of the country who laboured under adverse conditions of work. The first thing observed in the programmes was that workers in iron-ore, manganese-ore, limestone and dolomite-mines, who were generally attached to steel and cement plants and who were comparatively better organized, were also able to take better advantage of the available welfare facilities such as housing, water and scholarship. They were significantly ahead of their counterparts in the mica and beedi industry in this respect. Unionization and organization, therefore, seemed to make a difference in this regard.

The same workers, i.e. those in beedi and mica industry, also suffered much from diseases like T.B., scabbies, silicosis, respiratory diseases, chest diseases, water-born diseases like worms and diarrohea.

Quality of Life : Well-being of Workers Neglected

The welfare funds, as mentioned above, were established to cater to the needs of some of most neglected and unorganized workers. They were forced to work under very adverse conditions with low job and health security. The welfare interventions were expected to help them fight disease and destitution and to directly contribute to improving their quality of life. The effectiveness of the programmes had, therefore, to be judged in the context of this basic perspective.

The various welfare organizations were expected to help in implementing health, medical, minimum housing, water supply and educational programmes. As seen in Table 5.2, their main thrust was on creating medical (treatment) facilities, where the overall expenditure during the three-year period (1979-1982) ranged between 58.4 per cent (in mica) and 28 per cent (in limestone) of the total expenditure. Interestingly, least attention was paid (as shown by the expenditure pattern) to water supply, where the expenditure ranged from nil (in beedi) to 5.1 per cent (in limestone). Education (mostly scholarship) and nutrition (mid-day meal) also received scant attention where expenditure was only a small part of the budget for welfare facilities. The expenditure on administration ranged from 12 per cent (iron-ore) to about 17 per cent (mica) of the total budget.

TABLE 5.2 : Expenditure on Various Programmes (1978-79 to 1981-82) (as per cent of total expenditure)

Programmes	Labour Welfare Organizations			Beedi
	Iron/ Manganese-Ore	Mica	Limestone/ Dolomite	
Health and medical facilities	37	58	28	53
Housing	31	2	33	7
Water Supply	5	1	5	0
Other facilities	15	22	17	26
Administration	12	17	17	14

The health programme, despite receiving maximum attention in the budgetary allocation, did not succeed much in eliminating major diseases like T.B., scabbies, etc. The programme depended exclusively on curative and hospitalization approach ignoring the guidelines given in the national health policy (Ministry of Health, 1981), for preventive and promotive aspects. As is well known, and as recent campaigns against T.B. around the world have shown, little can be done in the face of widespread malnutrition. The destitute situation obtaining with our urban and rural poor is well known. For example, it was estimated (Gopalan, 1983) that out of 23 million children born in 1983, only 3 million would be able to grow into healthy, intellectually capable and productive citizens. The rest were doomed to either die or live with disease. The poor families suffering from malnutrition are forced to live in dark and airless slums, providing ideal conditions for tubercle bacillus and other deadly infections. With such quality of life, it was no wonder that the intended beneficiaries of the health welfare programme felt alienated and withdrawn.

The United Nations had earmarked the 1980s as the water decade. The goal was to provide hygienic water and sanitation for all by 1990. Launching the decade, the WHO Director-General had said, "I am utterly convinced that the number of taps per

1,000 population will be an infinitely more meaningful health indicator than the number of hospital beds per 1,000 population." Most infectious diseases in the Third World are water-borne, and 30,000 children die every day as a consequence of inadequate water or sanitation (ILO, 1984).

According to the national health policy, provision of potable water supply was pivotal to achieving the goal of health for all by A.D. 2000. It called for planned, coordinated and all out efforts in order to provide potable water to the entire rural population by the year 1990. It was, therefore, distressing to find the provision of water supply almost missing from the labour welfare programmes. The argument that this need was being attended to in the general development programmes was hardly credible. For that matter, health, housing, education and other needs also formed part of the minimum needs programme. The special welfare organizations were set up precisely because the vulnerable people, like mica and beedi and other such unorganized workers, did not have easy access to general facilities. They might have to wait for a long time, probably for their entire life and more, before such general facilities trickled down to them. They were in urgent need of special security arrangements. Many a time, their very survival depended upon security of such welfare interventions.

Greater Attention Needed for Labour Welfare

Formulation of a proper strategy for labour welfare for the organized workers was an urgent need for vitalizing the programmes. The following suggestions emerged from the reviews :

1. Community health programme is an integral part of the national health policy. It is also considered essential for family welfare. There was a need for greater attention to preventive aspects of health and for community education in this respect.
2. There was a need to pay urgent attention to developing adequate personnel policy for various functions in the labour welfare organizations.
3. There was a need for planned and properly designed training of various welfare personnel including medical personnel. They required reorientation for community health and education, social and preventive health

programmes and for developing a positive approach to the social aspects of health, housing and other welfare activities.

4. Education and housing were two other very vital needs which were practically ignored by the welfare organizations. The expenditure on housing was just 2 per cent for mica and about 7 per cent (of the total budget) for beedi workers. This neglect was tragic because these workers suffered from widespread and chronic ill-health and some minimum housing and education for their children and themselves could help to come out of the trap. The mica and beedi workers were more unorganized and poorer as compared to their counterparts in iron-ore and manganese-ore industry. They were, therefore, in need of special attention. Millions of beedi workers were scattered in all parts of the country and worked under most exploitative conditions, so much so that in some parts they were forced to mortgage their children (Mehta, 1983a). The organizations needed to show greater sensitivity and innovative approach in such cases.
5. People's participation in development is no more a mere rhetoric now. It is essential if public action mediated security networks have to succeed. People's self-actions could help release their self and social efficacy and help them to take charge of socio-economic matters (Mehta, 1983). Participation of the beneficiaries and their involvement in decision-making and implementation could make this into a people's programme.
6. Developing a people-orientation. The various organizations were set up as statutory and strategic interventions of public policy for the benefit of unorganized workers. Efforts, therefore, are needed to orient the organizations for welfare. Currently, they seem to be oriented more for administration and paper work. The case studies suggested that such organizations were highly centralized and followed a rigid code of rules and procedures. There was almost a total absence of even minimum delegation of powers. There was a lack of uniformity in personnel policy and job definition. Career incentives and promotional avenues were very inadequate.

It was, therefore, no wonder that the personnel, particularly the officials, showed 'bureaucratic' attitudes in their various functions. They were not able to show the required concern for the poorest for the poor who composed the unorganized workers. There was, therefore, a mismatch between objectives of the labour welfare organization and its administrative structure. As a result, vital goals like water supply, nutrition, housing and education suffered as the officials tended to give greater importance to rules and procedures than the service and welfare. The bureaucratic context of organization, as Korten and Unhoff (1981) have pointed out, tended to be reflected in the attitudes of the Staff. An organization which does not provide for participation of its own personnel in internal decision-making and in implementation cannot possibly hope to promote participation and well-being of the unorganized labour. Inside the public bureaucracy, the managers and other personnel themselves need to be empowered to empower people (Brinkerhoff, 1979).

There was, therefore, an urgent need for democratic reorientation and reorganization of the welfare functions. There was a need for more participation and people oriented structures. Community participation and public oriented health and other welfare programmes can be implemented successfully only with proper organizational structures and participatory management.

ANNEXURE 1

FUNCTIONS OF SECTIONS OF THE WELFARE WING OF THE MINISTRY OF LABOUR

Bonded Labour (BL) Section

Implementation of the Bonded Labour System (Abolition) Act, 1976, and the rules framed thereunder.
Implementation of the centrally sponsored scheme for the rehabilitation of freed bonded labourers.

Labour Welfare (LW) Section

Welfare of labour in public sector undertakings in the central sphere including labour welfare fund.
Industrial housing.
Civil pioneer force.
Labour cooperatives, consumers' cooperative stores and fair price shops.
Conditions of sweepers/rickshaw pullers/domestic servants/railway porters/licensed vendors.
Fair wage clause and contractors' labour regulations.
Contract Labour (Regulation & Abolition) Act, 1970.
Central Advisory Contract Labour Board.
Safety and health of workers in construction industry.
Matters relating to inter-state migrant labour.
Matters relating to casual labour.
Circus industry legislation.

Rural Workers' (RW) Section

Matters connected with rural unorganized labour.
Scheme to organize rural workers.
Legislative measures for agricultural labour, etc.

A – Welfare-I (Administration)

All service matters relating to appointment, transfer, fixation of pay, grant of leave, etc., relating to welfare commissioners, assistant welfare commissioners, welfare administrators, assistant welfare administrators, assistant engineer, accounts officer.

Administrative matters of audit cell.

Vigilance cases in respect of all officers of field labour welfare organization.

General complaints against welfare organization and officers.

Tour notes of welfare commissioners and follow-up action thereon.

Inspection reports of officers of the Ministry and their follow-up action.

Various administrative matters, viz creation of additional posts, hiring of office accommodation, telephone, etc., for the field officers.

B – Welfare-II (Administration)

Coordination.

Maintenance of reports, returns, etc.

Budgeting.

Matters relating to constitution and meetings of Central Advisory Committee under all welfare funds.

Matters relating to constitution, etc., of State Admisory Committees under all welfare funds.

Legislative matters relating to all the Welfare Acts and new legislative proposals.

Implementation of Beedi and Cigar Workers' (Conditions of Employment) act, 1966.

C – Welfare-III (Housing)

Housing schemes.

D – Welfare-IV (Non-priority)

Schemes relating to water supply, recreation, and education.

E – Welfare-V (Health)

Schemes relating to health under all welfare funds and I.L.O. projects, matters relating to medical officers.

F – Audit Cell

Matters relating to audit paras.
Matters relating to cess collection under different welfare funds.
Inspection of field offices.

6

PARTICIPATORY ADULT EDUCATION : Motivation for Organization and Collective Action

IT IS now well known that the gap between the rich and the poor tends to increase despite development. Development projects may benefit the rich more even though they may be intended to benefit the poor (Mukerjee, 1985). The rich and the powerful succeed in converting developmental opportunities to their advantage thereby further increasing their power. The development programmes have, therefore, to be viewed with reference to the entitlements accrued to the poor and the working people. The strategy and content of socio-economic programmes have to be examined in the context of the need to improve the quality of life of the disadvantaged people.

6.1. Development of Human Potential and Natural Resources

A significant characteristic of our situation is that we have resources needed for development, but these remain dormant in the absence of proper utilization. For instance, we are quite rich in human resources. Our people have sound common sense, intelligence, initiative and creativeness. Under unequal and oppressive socio-economic conditions, they are prevented from utilizing these assets to their advantage. They are forced into submission and are unable to take control and use the fruits of their own labour. Such adverse social environment curbs their capability and motivation to innovate and take risk.

It was estimated during the Sixth Five Year Plan that, between 1980 and 1995, the addition to the labour force would be 108 million persons. This came to 2.4 per cent per annum increase which was to be higher than the population growth (Planning Commission, 1981 : 21). However, the growth in population in urban areas, between 1983–1987-88 was 18.7 per cent, while the growth in employment was only 16.1 per cent. In the rural areas, the corresponding figures were 7.4 per cent and 4.1 per cent (*Economic Times*, 1991). The trends reflected the vital fact that while the population stock was becoming younger, with increased productive potential, the work opportunities for them were declining.

Implementation of Land Reforms

As stated repeatedly by the Planning Commission (1980), the objectives of the land reforms policy have been to remove impediments to development and to ensure quality of tenurial status and opportunity to all. Thus, the main elements of the land reforms policy have been fivefold, viz. (i) comprising regulation of rent, security of tenures and conferment of ownership rights to tenants (iii) ceiling on land holdings and distribution of surplus land; (iv) consolidation of holdings; and (v) compilation and updating of land records. In the emerging context of our socio-economic reality, the quality of life of our rural population cannot be improved without strict implementation of agricultural land ceiling and distribution of surplus land. The need for land reforms can hardly be over emphasized.

Education and Organization of Rural Workers

History of land reforms and redistribution of landed properties suggests that efforts have been more successful in areas where organized peasantry and landless workers have been able to generate pressures (Bandyopadhyaya, 1986). As discussed in Chapter 9, reforms achieved as a result of such organized and collective efforts not only help landless labour get land but they are also helped in acquiring and strengthening qualities of leadership, initiative and organization. The ILO Convention 141 (ILO, 1975) assumes importance in this context. India was among the first countries to ratify this convention. From time to time, the Planning Commission also has stressed the need for promoting organizations of rural workers so that a push for land reforms and for development could be generated by the people themselves.

As the National Literacy Mission (NLM) (Ministry of HRD, 1988) visualizes, appropriate educational strategies could help the people, at the grassroot level, to develop skills and readiness for organization for solving their problems. Review studies showed that efforts were required not only to provide adult literacy but also to impart education for increasing awareness and skills for problem diagnosis and action planning (Mehta, 1990, 1992). Such education could help promote organization of rural workers. As discussed in Chapters 8 and 9, through organized efforts, people were likely to demand their development entitlements. There was a need, however, for the people's own initiative in designing, implementing and managing development efforts. Adult education could help in developing and releasing such initiative.

Education and organization for rural workers also facilitate enforcement of social legislation, such as payment of minimum wages for agricultural labour, elimination of child labour and abolition and rehabilitation of bonded labour. Dependence on administrative efforts alone was counter-productive in this respect. In fact, many concerned bureaucrats were not even aware of the government policies in this regard. Many of those who were aware of such a policy (organization of rural workers) were apprehensive of "politics" and law and order problems. They were mostly negative towards the policy (Mehta, 1989). The people themselves, therefore, need to take initiative and make collective efforts for such social goals. The NLM also underlines the importance of people's initiative in this regard and calls for a total literacy campaign for mobilizing the illiterate poor for raising "demand" on the system (Ministry of HRD, 1991). Experience shows that uninvolved people, who are socially not conscious and assertive, are not able to take advantage of social development. For example, soon after their release the bonded labour relapse into bondage. The social and economic systems are so strongly against them that unorganized people are unable to confront them in a meaningful way.

6.2. Education for Rural Workers

People's development needs suggest certain specific objectives for adult education of the rural poor. These related to helping them to develop necessary skills, readiness and motivation for moving toward organizing themselves in various ways and for amelioration of their conditions. Not only their socio-economic conditions, but also their self-doubts and negative self-concepts inhibit their efforts for a dignified life. As suggested by the field functionaries and learners themselves (Mehta, 1990), it was necessary to integrate training and education to their specific economic social and human situation. In the following pages, we briefly describe such a training strategy implemented in a series of educational camps for the rural poor in different parts of the country during the 1975-83 period. It was not a usual literacy programme. Training camps were primarily geared to the objectives of awareness and organization. A typical programme was a five-day residential camp in which 50 or more rural workers, mostly from the scheduled caste and scheduled tribes, participated. The main objective, inputs and methods are briefly described below.

6.3. Objectives of Education and Training

Helping Participants Develop Participatory Skills

The need to motivate people for participation in developmental activities is now widely recognized (UNDP, 1993). However, some specific skills are needed for such effective participation. All the camp inputs were, therefore, designed to encourage the learners to participate more and more in various activities of the camp. In other words, instead of talking about the need for people's participation in development, the camp inputs were designed to provide an opportunity to the people to practice and develop participatory skills and to enable them to initiate efforts on their own.

From Individual to Collective Problem Diagnosis

As mentioned above, the camps were based on the assumption that participatory problem diagnosis was likely to promote readiness for organizing themselves. The rural poor are faced with so many problems. The training inputs sought to encourage them to open up and articulate their problems (and needs). First, they did this individually. Thereafter, they were encouraged to move from individual to collective problem diagnosis. The training process thus helped them understand that their individual problem was not only theirs but it was a part of a total social problem. In this learning process, the participants were helped to develop :

(i) Skills in group work,
(ii) Readiness for identifying one's own problem with those of the community, i.e. other poor like him/her and understanding community problems and his/her own.
(iii) Focus on community thinking and on community-ness, and
(iv) Skills in understanding and identifying important problems with a view to moving toward problem-solving and action-planning.

Weakening Dependency Syndrone : Increasing Sense of Efficacy and Assertion

Experience of working with rural poor and research in this regard suggested a long-drawn tendency in such people to depend on some significant others like government officials, moneylenders, landlords, etc. Such dependency syndrone was one of the major impediments in their efforts for organization. Promotion and sustenance of organizations require initiative, resourcefulness, action orientation, desire for improvement in the quality of individual and community life, hope of success, understanding their own strength and limitations, certain degree of personal and social awareness and above all realization that it was possible to develop effective organization for solving their various problems and for obtaining better living and working conditions. The training inputs were designed to develop and strength such a sense of social efficacy and assertion in the participants.

Promoting Concern for Social Achievement and Better Quality of Life

A heightened sense of influence and assertion was important in obtaining their rights and better quality of life. There was a need to arouse and reinforce such concerns and thoughts. Over the years, the rural poor have tended to learn not only a negative self-image, they have also tended to learn to *adapt* to low and degraded life. Such adaptation is obviously part of their unconscious strategy for survival under an extremely poor and dominative situation. Besides a sense of efficacy and influence, they needed to develop and reinforce a *concern* for better life and to include some sense of *success and achievement* for themselves. Training inputs were, therefore, designed in order to help participants move toward social achievement motivation for their own development. Details of conceptualization of such motivation have been reported elsewhere (Mehta, 1994).

Confidence for "Upward" Communication

The rural poor have to deal with a whole range of government officials, contractors, moneylenders, rich peasants/landlords and others. The structural conditions of their life and their dependency behaviour prevent them from badly confronting such elements. They also badly confronting such elements. They also probably lack confidence and skills in presenting their viewpoint and in "reading" various manipulations which others used on them. The training was, therefore, designed to bring about some kind of a thaw in their relationship with officials and to promote a sense of confidence in their interaction with them. Incidentally, the camp also provided an opportunity to the government officials to have first-hand information about grievances of the rural poor. Hopefully, such an opportunity and interactions helped the officials also to develop a more positive attitude towards problems of the rural poor.

6.4. The Training Strategy and Process

The training strategy was designed in pursuance of the educational objectives as discussed above. The principal goal was to help the participants enhance readiness, motivation, awareness and skills for developing and working in participatory organizations. For most of them, the camp was first such exposure. It was, therefore, essential to institute a process to draw them out of their timidity, shyness and a sense of cynicism. The various training inputs were designed, keeping in mind this overall objective. There were not many lectures. The faculty worked only as facilitators of the training process, designed to draw out the best from the participants. Some inputs and the training process thus generated are discussed below with one such camp as the focal point.

Briefing About the Camp Objectives : The Pre-Camp Survey

After the initial formalities, the facilitators made a brief presentation about the objectives of the training camp. Some of the participants were already, at least partially, aware of the objectives because of their contact with the field workers during the pre-camp survey. (Each camp was preceded by a survey of local needs, etc.). In fact some of the selected participants had helped in conducting interviews with the grassroot people in the field survey. In the process, they got briefed about the purpose of the pre-camp survey as well as about the camp itself. Such initial rapport and contacts were reinforced and a brief presentation was made at the outset in order to take the participants into confidence about the objectives of the camp. The participants were also briefed about the methodology of the camp. Thus, efforts were initiated to encourage the participants to become partners in conducting the camp.

Individual Work on Problems

After the initial briefing on the purpose of the camp, participants were encouraged to verbalize their problems and needs. The literate participants were encouraged to record some pressing problems faced by them in their daily life at home and at work. The illiterate participants were combined with their literate counterparts from the same village. Thus, the educated participants helped the rest of them to think about their various hardships and needs. First, more or less, they did this as an individual task without much interaction and discussion. Then they met in a plenary where some of them read out their individual record of problems. After some initial hesitation, several of them opened up and spoke out. As the participants listened to such reports, they began to appreciate certain communality in individual reports. At this stage a brief presentation was made to help them understand the common nature of their individual problems.

During the period of individual work, the facilitators provided a proforma to each participant. They answered questions regarding their schooling, size of their land holding, income, employment, indebtedness, etc. Some of the data thus obtained were later used in developing case studies and related reports. The proforma provided them with a common frame of reference and guided their thinking about the burning problems of employment, work, income, land, etc. (Mehta, 1983).

Small Group Discussions of Village Problems

The participants were now ready to discuss common problems which they faced in their everyday life. This was done in small groups of participants representing a cluster of adjoining villages. In each small group there were some educated participants. Even the illiterate ones were able to actively participate in such discussions. Each group recorded a summary of their main problems on a chart paper. These were then displayed for everyone to see. Someone from each of the groups reported the gist of their discussions to the entire group followed by clarifications and discussions. The facilitator helped them, while summarizing, to see a running commonness in such problems. Some specimen of such individual self-reports and some small group reports on village problems are given in Appendix I.

6.5. Problem Sensitivity of the People

Small group discussions revealed deep insights brought by the participants to the training programme. These were characterized by their rich experience replete with examples from daily life. They thus documented the wretched conditions of their life. They brought out their destitution and the strangulating grip of the village moneylenders and the traders. Table 6.1 shows a remarkable resemblance of their micro-level insights, as derived at this particular camp, held in early 1979, with some aspects of the national scene as derived from surveys and empirical research.

Grossroot Perceptions and the National Scene

It was not at all surprising to find a striking closeness between the problems perceived at the grassroot level and the picture obtaining at the national level. After all the poor faced these problems every day. Their perceptions included such vital problems as lack of food, chronic fear of starvation, no regular source of income and very low income, landlessness and worklessness, indebtedness, harassment and loot by shopkeepers and moneylenders, lack of drinking water and irrigation facility, harassment by the police, lack of hospital and medical facility, lack of schools as well as of adult education facility and lack of post office, roads and transport. It was interesting, as seen in Table 6.1, that the articulation of the poorest of the poor was a microcosm of the national scene. For instance, some national problems were : undernourishment of most of the people; some 40 per cent of the total population living under the poverty line at a monthly income of first Rs. 40 at 1972-73 prices giving less than Rs. 2 per day for more than three-forth of the rural population; the poorest 10 per cent of the rural households owning just 0.1 per cent and the richest 10 per cent owning more than half the total rural assets in 1971-72; millions of unemployed and underemployed in the rural areas; over 70 per cent of the rural population indebted; lack of drinking water in 80 per cent of our villages; 85 per cent of the country's population, mostly rural, going without any benefit from public health services; the prospect of millions of people becoming blind by the end of century due to malnutrition; over 70 per cent of the total population suffering from illiteracy with such numbers going up as the number of illiterate children in the age group 5-14 went up from 80 million in 1961 to 96 million in 1971.

Lack of Alternatives and Resistance

The young participants knew that the contractors, shopkeepers, money-lenders and others made a lot of money with the help of their labour. At one village, during the pre-survey, a Sarpanch, a 70-year-old Muslim small farmer-cum-social worker, described the exploitation of tribal labour as follows :

> One of the main forest products is tendu leaf for making beedis. All such products have been nationalized. The Forest Department asks for tenders each year. The usual rates are Rs. 45 per bag. The contractor is given half of it as off, i.e. Rs. 22.50 are taken from him for one bag of tendu leaves. The contractor uses the rest of the money for paying to the labourers and for meeting other expenditure. The labourers pick up the leaves and sell these to the contractor. The contractor, however, makes 6 to 7 lakh rupees just in one month in such transactions. After the tendu season is over, the local labourers have no other work. The illiterate tribals know about such profits by the contractor but are not

able to do anything. The forest officials are invariably in league with the contractor.

Same is the story about money-lending. The Sarpanch further reported that people mortgaged their things on a very high rate of interest (the money-lender would not give any loan without such mortgage). Interest of Rs. 10 per Rs. 100 per month is cut. The money-lenders used all kinds of tricks to prevent the return of the mortgaged ornaments even when the indebted person was ready to pay back the entire amount. They somehow continued to keep the debt so that it became time-barred. Thereafter the money-lender was free to swallow the ornaments. On the other hand, the tribal people thought it their moral duty to pay back the debt. They continued to pay back their debts even when these were legally liquidated (by the government) some years ago. The money-lenders were aware of the people's strong values and tradition. They fully cashed on the tribal morality.

Same was the case with all kinds of barter trading. For example, a shopkeeper would give 20 kgs of Jower (Coarse grain) in exchange of 20 kgs of urad or rice. The former was sold for Rs. 25, whereas the latter netted Rs. 50 in the market. The poor people knew that such trading was downright cheating but were not able to resist it. The training participants were able to verbalize and give many such instances at the camps. These patently illegal and exploitative practices continued unabated.

An interesting thing about such widespread exploitation of the rural poor, therefore, was that they knew that they were being fleeced by the money-lenders but were unable to resist such injustice and oppression. They also knew from experience, the consequences of individual resistance in the absence of appropriate alternatives. This was brought home to us during training in one of the Southern States, where bonded labourers had been "liberated" sometimes ago. The "freed" bonded labourers told us that they were happier under bondage with the landlord. After they were "liberated," the landlords refused to give them any work with the result that their conditions got worsened. As all means of production and work as well as sources of money-lending were controlled by the rural rich, individual resistance of such practices became counter-productive leading to greater harassment and opporession. Tolerance of gross injustice and humiliation, thus, becomes a strategy of survival in face of the all-powerful adversary.

TABLE 6.1 : Parallel between National Scene and Grassroot Level Perception of the Problems facing the Rural Poor

Grassroot Perception as Verbalized by the Poor	National Problems/Profile
1. Many times we don't have any food to eat. Sometimes forced to eat *chapatis* made of grass.	Minimum level of nutrition is inaccessible to over half the rural population and estimated 40 per cent of the urbans (Selbourne, 1977 : 19-23).
2. We don't have any regular income. Many times no income at all. The average income may not come even to Rs. 2.00 a day.	300 million people are estimated to be living below the poverty line at a monthly income of Rs. 40 at 1972-73 prices. The average per capita income stands more or less at Rs. 2.50 daily as stated officially in Oct. 1978. This works out at less than Rs. 2 a day for more than 3/4th of the population living in rural areas (*ibid* : 24-29).
3. Many of us have no land, some of us have some land, but mostly hilly and not fertile.	The poorest 10 per cent of the rural households owned 0.1 per cent and the rich 10 per cent owned more than half the total rural assets in 1971-72. The percentage of landlessness increased from 19 per cent in 1961 to 31 per cent in 1971 (Raj Krishna).
4. There is practically no work or employment for us in villages. Some of us are engaged in food-for-work construction activity. This is also irregular. Most people have to be away from their homes for 6 to 8 months in search of work.	There are some 20.5 million unemployed persons—16.5 million in rural areas and 4 million in urban areas (Rajkrishna, 1978).
5. Shopkeepers and money-lenders loot us all the time. We are forced into indebtedness at very high rates of interest. Even Cooperative Credit Societies force us to give a receipt for Rs. 500 to Rs. 700 for a loan of Rs. 400.	Apart from millions of destitute unemployed landless rural poor who are indebted, 65 per cent to 70 per cent of small and marginal land-holders are indebted for amounts ranging from Rs. 250 to Rs. 500. The average amount of debt in the agricultural labour households increased from Rs. 148 in 1964-65 to Rs. 387 in 1974-75 and 48 per cent of such debts were provided by money-lenders in 1974-75 whereas it was 31 per cent in 1964-65 (Selbourne, *op cit.* : 37-38).

6. Facility for irrigation does not exist. Even drinking water facility is not there. There are some wells with *kaccha pani* (temporary and shallow water). Several wells are half-dug and are non-functional out of order.	Besides widespread malnutrition, there is a lack of drinking water in 80 per cent of India's villages (*ibid* : 104-105).
7. We have practically no hospital and medical facility. We have to carry out sick persons physically on our shoulders, crossing rivers and hills to the Tehsil hospital, where also there is only one doctor. Our sick people die without treatment.	According to the ICMR, hardly 15 per cent of the country's population derives benefit from our public health services. According to WHO's warning, there will be 20 million blind people in India by the end of the century.
8. We don't have even primary schools in several of our villages. At some places there are schools without building and teachers. Our children are frequently driven out of the school by the teachers for want of proper dress, etc.	The number of illiterate children in the age group 5-15 went up from 80 million in 1961 to 97 million in 1971. One in every two children dropout of class I in the rural areas (Naik, 1975).
9. We don't have any facility for adult education in our villages.	71 per cent of the total population and 81 per cent of the women are illiterate. Nearly half the illiterate population of the world live in India (*ibid*).

* Based on a consensus in small group discussions by some 60 young somewhat educated tribal (Bhils) participants of an Education Camp held at Kotra Chhavni in Udaipur district of Rajasthan, February 3-8, 1979.

Story-writing : Discussion and Analysis

Individual work and group discussions helped the participants learn problemitization which enabled them to open up. Their initial shyness receded gradually and they were ready to ask questions. They then actively participated in various training tasks. At this stage (at some training camps, depending on the situation) they were involved in a story writing exercise. They were provided with a set of pictures and a story-writing booklet. They saw a picture for a few seconds and then wrote a story in the booklet. The illiterate participants were separately helped by the facilitators to tell a story after seeing the picture. This was recorded. After the story-writing was over the participants were eager to know the purpose of the exercise. They were then encouraged to read out their stories so that the purpose could be clarified. Several of them volunteered and read aloud. The facilitator helped them to understand some of the goals in the story. Their attention was drawn to the content and nature of their thoughts as revealed in the stories. Do they think about improving their living and working conditions? Do they think about providing good education to their children, to get better training for themselves; stable work for themselves; think about improving living conditions in the village? Do they think how they can solve their problems? Do they think of influencing the on-going situation in order to solve some of their problems and to overcome difficulties created by the establishment, money-lenders and others? Or do they feel helpless and reconciled to their poor conditions of life and work? They were gradually helped to understand the importance of these various goals and thoughts. As stories were being read, conceptual clarifications were provided. The individual and group problems verbalized earlier were used to illustrate the various points. Thoughts in the stories and the thoughts as contained in their various perceived problems were compared and put together in order to bring out the importance of their ideas and dreams (for conceptual details of story analysis, see Mehta, 1994; Appendix I).

Generating Experiences by Simulated Games

In between small group discussions and story analysis, the participants were involved in a series of games. These were introduced specifically to generate experience of competitive and collaborative situations; individual and collective action; and personal and group goals for problem solving. They got actively involved in these games both for fun and for meaningful learning from group interactions and the results of the games. The data were analyzed to facilitate appropriate learning. This was done with particular reference to the need and importance of collective action, teamwork and participatory organizations. The experience thus obtained was integrated with the ideas generated via stories, small group discussions and problemitization.

Awareness about Legal and Other Rights

Participating in talks, discussions and exercises, they became aware of various protective laws and rights bestowed on them by the laws of the land. They discussed such issues and became aware of their right to form associations and organizations, get them registered, demand minimum wages; refuse to serve as a bonded labour; refuse doing any kind of *begar* (work without any remuneration) for anyone; to get medical facility; schooling for children, a small piece of land for a house; membership of various cooperative societies and so on.

Interface with Officials

Toward the fourth day of the training camp, the participants interacted with some concerned government officials particularly those operating at the district level such as the Block Development Officer, tribal development officials, project officers and sometimes also police officials. Such an interface between the participants and the officials helped the "excluded" (i.e. the rural poor) to question the officials responsible for various development activities. It was an experience for the facilitators to see the rural poor effectively questioning the government officials on various issues. They asked them searching questions and gave them concrete cases of injustice and atrocities committed on the villagers. On their part, the government officials, briefed in advance, also tried to come up to the level of the challenge thus posed by the participants. They were candid in giving information about various development activities and their legal rights about wages, etc. While giving such information, they invited the participants to collaborate with them in implementing various development schemes. They asked them to continue contacts with them and to bring to their notice by meeting personally or by writing any unjust acts committed on them in future. They assured help and cooperation with the efforts to solve some of the problems. They also offered assistance in getting their association registered and in preparing a constitution if they so desired.

From Individual to Community Sensitivity

It could be perceived, as the various camp inputs unfolded, that the participants gradually moved from personal problems and goals to larger problems and issues. This helped to imbibe group and social sensitivity about such problems and issues. Their attention gradually got focuseed on the need for improving living and working conditions by personal and collective action backed by awareness of personal and social phenomena and a sense of optimism in facing and overcoming their problems.

6.6. Releasing the Need for Organizing

As the training moved further, the participants developed problem-solving skills and a sense of efficacy. They also began to perceive the need for unity and organization among themselves. Such a need was expressed in various ways such as in group discussions, individual reporting, writing of stories and experience generated in other games and exercises. They began to realize the importance of organizing themselves in some form or the other. They recalled the importance of collective strengths and social action in various ways in meeting with their problems and in solving them. Thus, a young participant in one of the education camps, responding to a thematic picture, wrote :

> "After removing difficulties ourselves we would stand on our own feet and live in happiness. In order to bring such a situation for ourselves we should walk together and from an organization and work together. As long as we sit like dumb people painful conditions continue in life. For removing them we should work together in the society. I imagine that if we think and then work we can get happiness in life. For raising the economic conditions of our area, i.e. for removing our difficulties and sorrows, we should work unitedly send boys to school for education so that they become able after getting education."

Participation in Education

There has been a widespread realization, as discussed in Chapter 9, that the process of development could be very much accelerated by promoting participation of the concerned people in designing, implementing and managing such activities. Education designed to promote such participation itself cannot be conducted in a non-participative way. The traditional classroom instruction where teachers talk and others listen may not be conducive to adult education. This itself has to become participatory where learners are active partners in the process of educating themselves. Newer educational methods are obviously needed here. The process, methods and content of education cannot be separated from the intended objectives of education, particularly in the context of development activities. The concerned rural poor themselves have to take the initiative in such matters. Some experience of the concerned adult learners and their instructors in this respect are discussed elsewhere (Mehta, 1990).

Participatory Non-formal Education

As mentioned above, the young camp participants perceived the need for education, including adult education as well as need for employment and income generating activities for themselves. That mere school education did not help the rural people was graphically described by Ramlal, a 20-year-old Bhil boy, educated up to class V, while inaugurating one of the training programmes. He said :

> "The family gave education to one boy. Incurred expenditure. The boy passed class X, he has no job now. The family had thought that he would get a good job, bring money by which they would purchase cloth. Others were doing agriculture to get grain for the family. Took a loan for this boy's education. Took more loan. Now the Seth (money-lender) wants his money back. Forced to give him grain...leaving less to eat. Have to go to the forest to bring wood to meet daily needs. All this is not sufficient to meet the needs. Now reduced to starvation. Many a time there are only vegetables to eat. Sometimes this is also not available."

In the absence of work opportunities, hopes of the poor family are dashed to the ground. They develop a feeling that education has brought them only indebtedness and unemployment. They, thus, become cynical about adult education and see no purpose in it. It illustrates the need for integrated education with components for socio-economic awareness and vocational skills. Such education should promote employment, break their isolation and motivate them to participate in social and public activities.

The adult educators and others involved in such activities could, at best, play the role of facilitators of this process and as resource persons for various content inputs. Participation in the process of education is vital in adult literacy as it cannot be separated from life problems and needs of the learners—in this case the rural poor. The more they become aware of the deeper socio-economic problems and develop readiness for confronting such problems, more motivated they become to take part in people's movement for education and development (Mehta, 1990).

Self-initiated Organized Action Essential for Implementation

Adult education and organization of rural workers could play an important role in socio-economic programmes, particularly anti-poverty and social development programmes. People's own action, and more so when it is organized social action, could go a long way in enforcing and obtaining a minimum wage, rehabilitation of bonded labour and child labour and in initiating, sustaining and managing sustainable development projects, as discussed in Chapter 8. Such programmes were likely to be resisted by vested interests (Chandra and Metha, 1984; Mehta, 1983). Without organization and a collective strategy, rural workers are not able to resist such unjust practices. Rural labour camps and other adult educational activities could play an important role in creating awareness, preparedness, motivation and skills for problem diagnosis, action planning and organization among the rural workers. Such activities could help in inculcating capability and as sense of competence and enable the poor to move toward amelioration of their situation and to improve their quality of life entitlements.

7

ISSUES IN ORGANIZATION OF THE POOR: A Case Study of some Non-Government Efforts

INDIA was one of the first countries to ratify the ILO convention 141 which enjoins that it shall be the objective of the national policy concerning rural development to facilitate the establishment and growth of strong and independent organizations of rural workers. Successive Five Year Plans have underlined the importance of involvement of rural workers organizations as essential for "ensuring the benefits intended for rural workers under various development programmes." Noting further that it will take time for voluntary agencies and trade unions to make a dent among these sections, it was considered, "necessary for the State machinery to facilitate the process in the initial stages." (Planning Commission, Sixth Five Year Plan, 1980 : 17).

Involvement of Non-Government Organizations

Voluntary organizations, social action groups and others have, however been, active on their own in working with people at grass-root level. Some of them have been active in mobilizing the rural poor with a view to promoting their organization in order to help them derive their entitlements. Taking advantage of a government scheme, some NGOs got involved in systematic training and mobilization activities with a view to promoting awareness and organizing skills among grassroot level workers in order to facilitate organization of beneficiaries of the anti-poverty programme.[1]

7.1. The Case Study

The present case study is based on a sample review of the functioning of the above government scheme. This study was conducted in four states, namely, Madhya Pradesh, Rajasthan, Bihar and Uttar Pradesh, in order to understand the impact of the various activities undertaken by some voluntary agencies for organization of beneficiaries of the anti-poverty programme. The concerned agencies[2] were engaged in wide-ranging activities for preparing the rural poor to assert for getting their rightful benefits. They had identified beneficiaries; undertaken surveys of the local needs, examined official documents to correlate development projects with the needs of the beneficiaries; and organized training and large group camps to make the beneficiaries aware of various development benefits.

Preparatory Work

Besides undertaking surveys of needs and for identification of beneficiaries in the pre-camp field work, the voluntary agencies conducted mass contacts and discussions to prepare the ground for awareness camps and training courses. Such pre-camp activities helped them not only to understand the local needs and problems but also in identifying any actual potential leaders among the rural poor. They used this opportunity to explain the Scheme and to educate the potential beneficiaries about the need for organization. As a result, their interest was aroused and later, a large number of people joined the voluntary agency concerned to participate in camps and training courses. Thus, the preparatory field work motivated the beneficiaries for participating in the Scheme

7.2. Training Activities

Awareness Camps

In pursuance of the programme for organizating the rural poor, various voluntary organization undertook several kinds of activities including training and awareness camps. The content, methods and duration of such training varied from organization to organization. All such training camps, however, sought to inform the beneficiaries about various schemes and benefits under the anti-poverty programme. As per the government schemes, all agencies involved various government officials in such camps with a view to bringing them face to face with the beneficiaries. Some training camps, such as those held at Govindpur (U.P.), Khajuti (Rajasthan) and Phulwari Sharif (Bihar) involved the participants in discussing and reflecting on issues pertaining to socio-economic exploitation and poverty. They thus helped them to see the need for an organization. Some other voluntary agencies remained confined largely to imparting vocational and/or health information.

Tendency to Lecture

The voluntary agencies involved in promoting organization of the rural poor differed widely in their attention to developing awareness and inculcating skills for organizing in their training efforts. On the whole, awareness camps organized in this respect were rather weak on this primary objective itself. Methodologically, they tended to "lecture" the beneficiaries about virtues of organization without involving them in reflection and action in this respect. Government officials' lectures about anti-poverty schemes and various economic gains available to the poor tended to reinforce their habitual expectation of subsidies and loans. Such lectures did inform them about procedures, etc., for getting such benefits. Some of the participants were later able to use their contact with the officials to get some projects sanctioned. However, such personal gains were obtained with the help of recommendation and contacts rather than collectively with the help of their organization. In this sense, their tendency to "depend" on the officials and others tended to be reinforced.

Inputs and Methods

Although most of the training programmes were dominated by lectures, some agencies did effectively use group discussions, processions, cultural activities, exhibitions and mass rallies as training methods for promoting consciousness. Such attempts, however, were only very few. But such inputs helped the participants overcome some of their fears and open up to raise questions about the anti-poverty programme.

Some agencies were already active in mobilizing the rural poor in discussing and analyzing local problems pertaining to their land entitlement, court cases and judgements about land ownership, issues relating to bonded labour, child labour, problems of water, health, sanitation, education, public distribution of essential commodities, payment of minimum wages, public corruption, police behaviour and such other local matters. Such issues as were closely linked with their daily experience made sense to them and so evoked keen interest among the beneficiaries. Such "activist" agencies, therefore, established quick rapport with the poor. They brought such experience and inputs to their training camps.

Talking and Doing

As mentioned above, while voluntary agencies and social action groups were active in preparing the rural poor for participating in interventions and organizing themselves, most of them, however stopped at informing them about development projects. Information unbacked by appropriate individual and collective action tended to develop grievance orientation among the poor. This was found at all places and the beneficiaries came out with a large number of problems during the review discussions and interviews. They articulated problems concerning water, employment, etc. Women were found to be equally, if not more, active in this respect. However, with such articulation of needs, they expected others including government and non-government officials to oblige and solve their problems. At places where voluntary agencies were active in involving people in organizing themselves, the rural poor were able to take a step further. They were able to initiate action for problem solving and link it with their own efforts and organization. But they were not so skilful in planning and organizing, no were they clear about strategies for obtaining access to entitlements. They were, however, enthusiastic and active. Experience suggests that whenever people were activated to assert for problem-solving their motivation for organization as well as education was aroused and strengthened.

7.3. Mobilization and Participation

Social Learning for Interventions

The above experience, notably at Khajuri, Govindpur and Phulwari Sharif, illustrated the importance of mobilization of people for appropriate interventions. People at these places were involved in not only discussing issues concerning water, corruption, land, etc., but they actually participated in collective action for procuring justice and their entitlements. Interestingly, such "active" beneficiaries were also able to obtain greater benefits under the anti-poverty programme. During the Review, such beneficiaries recalled their own success in this connection and articulated the importance of organization. It, thus, appeared that awareness camps and training were more effective in motivating the poor when these were preceded and followed by mobilization for action. Such beneficiaries were able to exercise influence upwards for initiating a process of two-way communication towards decentralized management of development programmes. Such beneficiaries were able to perceive the importance of their own initiative and efforts for improving their conditions of life. They also revealed some sense of belonging with their respective voluntary agencies. They thought these were their own organizations.

Formation of Groups : Organization

Despite varying emphasis on action for organization, the voluntary agencies, by and large, helped the rural poor to come together, interact with each other and form some kind of groups. The nature of such groups varied from place to place. For example, at some places they grouped together to talk about their health problems; at some they talked about different vocational trades and at some others they came together to elect representatives to form some village-level collective. However, mobilization and collective action facilitated group formation to become an integral part of the process of empowerment. At such places, the people were able to relate smaller groups to their large organization and also talk about the importance of organization in bettering their lives. Such voluntary agencies which were able to inculcate awareness about the importance of unity and organization were also able to motivate the people for active participation in various campaigns and interventions. In such cases, people saw a meaning in their being members of groups and organizations. They perceived such activities as purposive and useful. The experience, therefore, suggested that mobilization provides a motivational link for activizing the poor for collective action and organization. Such mobilization provides a base for promoting people's participation in decentralized management of development. At such places, people were able to talk, reflect and assert for problem-solving. They, in turn, activized the administration and, in some cases, forced them to act in their favour. They became a force of vigilance against corrupt practices.

Emerging Readiness for Organization

Thus, it was interesting to find that there was a felt need for collective action for improving quality of life almost everywhere and the voluntary agencies were active in promoting organization. This was clearly perceived at almost all the places during the review discussions and interviews. This was also perceived even at places where the given voluntary agency was not that active in this regard. At some places, the agencies concerned were interested only in preventive health care and sanitation. There also, the rural poor, both men and women, recalled their needs and problems and showed readiness for collective action and organization. They talked about the need for employment, payment of minimum wages, facilities for drinking water, schools, etc., although these issues were not at all discussed by the voluntary agencies in their camps, etc.

The experience here, therefore, suggested that participation and united action for improving any segment of conditions of life probably has a spread effect and the beneficiaries are able to see and articulate their other problems which are in any case uppermost in their minds. Such activities helped in inculcating and strengthening their concern for better quality of life, thus motivating them for participation in organizations and collective action. They also begin to articulate the need for "confronting" the local administration and the panchayats for their rightful entitlements. Thus, formation of groups and group action and participation in any segment of social development tended to educate the people for a better quality of life. Such a concern further motivated them for organized and collective action. Such participation thus paved the way for promoting organization of the poor.

Local Bureaucracy not Ready

One of the principal objectives of the scheme for promoting organization of beneficiaries was to help them use appropriate strategy for obtaining their rightful entitlements. As mentioned above, development officials were invited to awareness camps form time to time to provide information about various projects. However, the experience suggested that such delivery of information was not enough unless it was put into action. It tended to heighten the expectations of the beneficiaries which were not fulfilled in practice. Such talks, therefore, reinforced the perceived split between promise and practice and created dissonance in the minds of the beneficiaries. Most people failed to get any benefit while some others had to face humiliating hardships in getting some limited benefits. The result, therefore, was a deep sense of disillusionment about anti-poverty programmes. As a result, people's faith in government was weakened and created a serious problem of credibility.

Communication Upward : Feedback to Administration

Another important objective of inviting government officials to the awareness camps, etc., was to provide them with meaningful feedback. This could result in a two-way communication process. Such a feedback could enable the administration to improve functioning of various programmes. In reality, however, this did not seem to happen. There was not much upward communication. In fact, officials were not ready to accept such feedback as they did not show any concern for improving their own functioning and effectiveness. Their interest probably lied somewhere else.

Promise and Practice : The Widening Gap

As mentioned above, attitudes of officials including some elected representatives tended to reinforce the gap between promise and reality. While activities of some of the voluntary agencies heightened expectation and awareness among the poor, the administration remained largely non-responsive. People became more "demanding", as could be expected, while the officials tended to keep distance from them. In fact, this process provided reverse feedback to the people about the functioning of the administrative machinery and in some cases, local panchayat institutions. For example, they came face to face with the malfunctioning of rural banks, primary schools (under Panchayat

Samitis) and such other institutions. They became much more conscious of the malpractices.

7.4. The Rising Expectations and Disillusionment

Training, awareness camps and other activities raised hope of the participants. These were, however, frustrated by the non-responsive administration. The resultant dissonance was quite deep. This was quite clear at all places during the review when the beneficiaries articulated their needs and problems. In fact they expressed a sense of deep hurt about lack of employment, lack of water and irrigation, about public corruption and police harassment, etc. At some places, the beneficiaries had not even heard of any anti-poverty programme in their areas. They, therefore, felt disappointed and angry. The picture was more or less the same at all places. The message was clear. They were not at all happy with the implementation of development programmes and with the treatment they were receiving at the hands of local elite.

Dissonance and Attitudinal Change : Learning to Organize and Intervene

The heightened awareness accompanied by resultant dissonance motivated beneficiaries to participate in organized interventions. There was, therefore, a significant change in their traditional dependency behaviour. Instead of looking up to the officials and other influential persons, they were somewhat ready now to act along with other people. This was evident at places like Govindpur, Khajuri and Phulwari Sharif. Success of participation and self-action there taught them the benefits of organizing efforts, thus, further reinforcing their desire for organization and collective action. Self-action strengthened their confidence and helped them overcome their individual fears. Weakening of dependency and fears facilitated learning to organize and intervene. However, at some other places, they tended to transfer their dependency on government officials to non-government officials hoping that the latter would use their influence to get them some benefits. The change from "dependency" to "self-action" seemed to occur only when voluntary agencies mobilized them, trained and helped them to take initiative and participate in interventions.

7.5. Mobilization and Organization

Some Gains Obtained

Using a variety of methods with varying degrees of success, the grassroot level agencies were able to help achieve several important gains for the poor by implementing some programme of mobilization, education and organization. Some such gains have already been described above. These can be summarized as follows :

1. *Organization : Groups Formed*

The beneficiaries were helped to form themselves into several kinds of groups. Group formation helped them in taking collective action with regard to some of their problems.

2. *Sense of Disillusionment*

Awareness camps and follow-up experience helped sharpen their sense of dissonance between expectation and reality. The resultant sense of disillusionment and frustration reinforced their motivation for organization and interventions.

3. *Activist Role*

As a result of such motivation, some of the beneficiaries actually got involved in planning and implementing collective strategies for obtaining their entitlements. There was some movement from passivity to activity—from being the "object" of development to becoming the "subject" and actor in the process. In some cases, they were able to gain some tangible economic benefit from some anti-poverty programme.

4. *Empowerment : Sense of Efficacy*

Cumulatively, the most striking gain was a perceptible movement in empowerment of the beneficiaries. One of the most important objectives of organization of the rural poor was to help them gain a sense of efficacy. Traditionally, the rural poor have been afraid of known and unknown things. They were not able to speak out. The present programme made significant difference in this situation. At all the places, the beneficiaries, including women, gave evidence of their power of articulation. They were no longer so much afraid. Their desire to speak out was certainly heightened.

5. *Ready to Get Organized*

There was enough evidence to suggest that the beneficiaries were ready to get organized. Formation of groups, disillusionment with implementation of anti-poverty programmes, awareness, emergence of activist role and their enhanced sense of efficacy and confidence – all helped them to get a feel of empowerment. Such objective and subjective changes strengthened their motivation and readiness for unity and organization.

7.6. Organization of the Poor

Some Emerging Issues

Analysis of experience relating to implementation of the government scheme of promoting organization of beneficiaries of anti-poverty programmes, as briefly discussed above, suggested several important issues. Understanding of such issues could be helpful to those engaged in empowering and organizing people. Some such issues could be briefly summarized as follows :

1. *Information is not Enough*

Imparting of information about anti-poverty programmes and other related development activities is important but not enough. Talks by officials do not produce the desired interface between development administration and beneficiaries. The officials tend to behave in their usual way, i.e. "*talking to people*" and not "*talking with people*."

2. *Administration not Oriented*

The above experience brings out the well-known fact that the administrative machinery as well as the local bodies and Panchayati Raj institutions are not geared and oriented to help the poor. Motivationally and attitudinally, the officials tend to keep distance from the people. They tend to look down upon them and act against their interest. A variety of hardships and blocks are thus created.

3. *Mobilization and Interventions Help*

The experience shows the importance of mobilization of people's movements and planned interventions. Such activities help enhance and enrich awareness of the people and prepare them for action. Mere awareness camps are not enough in this respect. They have to be preceded and followed by purposeful mobilization and mass campaigns.

4. *Awareness Enhance Articulation*

Increasing awareness enhances articulation of grievances. Participation in awareness camps help them articulate their grievances, both individually and collectively. This also results in certain collective representations to the local administration. Such articulation of grievances could become an effective means of communication and feedback.

5. *Women Getting Activized*

Barring one or two places, women were actively involved in various activities implemented by the voluntary agencies. At some places, women appeared to be more militant than men. One of the significant changes observed was women articulating "demands" for education, health care and other such facilities. They also now talked about employment and proper wages. They were active in demonstrations and interventions. It was obvious that women were getting activized. The programme for organization of the poor contributed to this emerging process of women's militacy. This can be a significant factor in an effective people's movement for decentralization, education and development.

6. *Administrative Corruption*

One of the most frequent and common issues binding the poor together at all the places was their articulation of administrative corruption and harassment. At several places, they named the officials and "brokers," giving concrete instances of corruption and malpractices. Bank officials came in for severe indictment by the people. Mobilization and participation in collective strategies and interventions was successful, at least in some cases, in confronting and preventing such corruption. However, this is a very widespread well entrenched phenomenon with strong linkages with the entrenched power structure. This is likely to be a very powerful hindering factor in organization and participation.

7. *Sense of Helplessness as well as Determination*

The people continued to express their sense of helplessness in the face of widespread administrative corruption. At the same time, there was, however, some indication of an emerging sense of determination to confront and overcome this situation. The role and potential of organization of the people in weakening and checking administrative and political corruption and in effective decentralized development can hardly be over-emphasized.

7.7. Suggested Action

The experience suggested the need for the following actions for promoting, strengthening and sustaining organization of the people toward an effective development and removal of poverty and destitution. The government scheme (under the Council for Advancement of People's Action and Rural Technology (CAPART) for promoting organization of the rural poor, accordingly, needs further strengthening.

1. *Orientation of Administration*

There is a need for suitably designed awareness camps and training courses for government officials, elected officials and other implementing personnel to promote a more effective interface with the poor. Such officials should be exposed to searching questions and the wrath of the people in a friendly climate of learning and collaboration. Such an exposure and feedback could help re-educate them and develop pro-people and participatory orientation in them.

2. *Capacity Building for Voluntary Agencies*

A large number of voluntary agencies have shown interest in implementing the government scheme. Many of them have been doing valuable work in this regard. However, educational tasks such as mobilization, training, follow-up activities, interventions, etc. need a systematic approach. Such activities need to be properly designed and implemented for maximum effectiveness. These in turn require specific skills and orientations among the voluntary agencies themselves. There is a need to undertake "internal" development; training of trainers; preparation of reading and training materials, etc., in this connection.

3. *Enriching the Programme Content*

Training programme inputs for animators, trainers and officials involved in promoting organization of the poor required attention. For example, there was a need to pay attention to the following : Sense of vigilance and pro-active orientation for anticipating and resolving conflicts; planning and conducting mass mobilization and interventions; economic and social understanding of issues pertaining to minimum wages, administrative and public corruption, child and mother care, education, etc; concepts and skills relating to organization of the rural poor, people's participation, decentralization and democratization of development programmes, etc.; designing and conducting training courses; preparation of reading and training materials, motivating and preparing the poor for promoting organization and for their effective functioning.

4. *Integration with National Literacy Mission and Other Development Programmes*

There was a significant and desirable overlap between the scheme for organization of beneficiaries of anti-poverty programmes (for example as administered by CAPART under the Ministry of Rural Development) and objectives of the National Literacy Mission (as administrated by the Department of Education, Ministry of HRD) and other related development programmes. For example, one of the goals of the National Literacy Mission (NLM) is to help the poor "become aware of the causes of their deprivation and move towards amelioration of their conditions through organization and participation in the process of development."

Steps are, therefore, required, to in-build this overlap in the Scheme itself. In this respect, Jan Shikshan Nilayums (under the NLM) could be helpful in promoting organization of the beneficiaries.

5. *Defining Tangible and Intangible Gains*

It would be helpful to define some important tangible gains of the Scheme such as benefits under anti-poverty programmes and, more importantly, the expected subjective changes and skill development. For instance, the Scheme seeks to develop motivation and skills for promoting and running organizations. These skills and expected changes need to be properly defined. This would also help in bringing about clarity in the programmes and help achieve desired results in a meaningful way.

6. *Monitoring and Consulting Help*

Fulfilment of the above mentioned tasks and effective implementation of the programme of organization of the poor require continuous monitoring and consulting help. Capability of the agencies concerned further develops as they acquire experience of implementing the Scheme. Experience, however, could be converted into learning and development when effective monitoring and consulting help are available at all stages and to all the personnel and agencies concerned.

7. *Documentation of Experience*

Over the years, voluntary agencies and other organizations have accumulated rich experience of promoting education and organization of the poor. There are significant success stories as well as failure experience. These need to be meaningfully documented. Such documentation is likely to yield useful case studies and basic teaching-learning materials including films, which would be useful not only in the effective implementation of this programme but also in fulfilment of the goals of the National Literacy Mission and similar other social development programmes.

7.8. Concluding Remark

The review of the functioning of the government Scheme for promoting organization of beneficiaries of anti-poverty programmes yielded rich information. Despite shortcomings, the implementing agencies succeeded in generating considerable awareness among the beneficiaries and in motivating them for efforts at organizing themselves. The programme has potential for promoting education and organization of the poor and for facilitating people's participation in development and in their struggles for better living conditions.

NOTES

1. The Council for People's Action and Rural Technology (CAPART) has been implementing a Scheme for promoting organization of the beneficiaries of the anti-poverty programme. The Council has sanctioned a large number of projects to voluntary agencies to this effect. The programme seeks to promote knowledge about development programmes and encourages formation of action groups and effective interaction between the beneficiaries and officials implementing development programmes. It seeks to heighten awareness of the beneficiaries about their entitlements and to help them develop strategies and assertion for obtaining such entitlements.
2. A review of the functioning of the Scheme was undertaken in four States, namely, Rajasthan, Madhya Pradesh, Bihar and Uttar Pradesh. It involved case studies of programmes as being implemented by seven voluntary agencies. These agencies were : Vidya Bhavan Society (Krishi Vigyan Kendra, Udaipur, Rajasthan); Gram Vikas Samiti (Khajuri, Rajasthan); PRAYAS (Phulwari Sharif, Bihar); Badalo Foundation (Dumka, Bihar); Society for Agro-Industrial Education in India (Moradabad, Uttar Pradesh); Banwasi Sewa Ashram (Sonebhadra, Uttar Pradesh) and Bahai's Vocational Institute for Rural Women (Indore, Madhya Pradesh).

8

ORGANIZING PEOPLE FOR EDUCATION AND DEVELOPMENT

DESPITE the stated goal of poverty alleviation, the gap between the rich and the poor has, however, tended to widen in several developing countries (ILO, 1977 : ESCAP, 1982; Planning Commission, Sixth Five Year Plan, 1980). The poor, particularly the rural poor, have not even been able to derive their specific entitlements from development plans. The powerful rich sections of the society have managed to divert benefits for themselves, thereby further increasing their power. One of the reasons for this and the failure of the poor to assert in this respect is that they are largely scattered and unorganized. It was precisely for this reason that the International Labour Organization adopted their Rural Workers Organization Convention, 1975 (No. 141) which recognize that "the importance of rural workers in the world makes it urgent to associate them with economic and social development action if conditions of work and life are to be permanently and effectively improved". (ILO, 1982 : 15). The Convention further states that "it shall be an objective of national policy concerning rural development to facilitate the growth and voluntariness of strong and independent organizations of rural workers" (Article 4). The ILO's earlier Recommendation No. 127 concerning the role of cooperatives in economic and social development in the developing countries (ILO, 1982a; 151-157) calls for voluntary association of people to achieve a common and democratically controlled and independent organization.

8.1. Empowerment of People

Despite the ILO recommendations and conventions and the fact that several developing countries including India has duly ratified these conventions, such policies have largely remained on paper. Studies show that majority of the senior Central Government officials responsible for poverty alleviation programmes were not even aware of these conventions. Those who were, thought that, sections of political parties and civil servants were not only indifferent to organization of the poor but actually came in the way of such a policy (Mehta, 1989). It is obvious that organizing the poor is a difficult and politically charged and controversial matter.

The vested interests entrenched in the socio-economic system strongly resist any efforts at organizing the poor. Not only such opposing forces strongly inhibit the process of organizing the poor but even the poor themselves have learnt over the years to doubt their own capabilities. They have internalized a negative self-image of themselves. Such social learning is based on a realistic assessment of the power of their adversaries. In this process, however, they learn to explain their explcitation by doubting themselves. (Elias and Scotson, 1965). The exploited people are driven to learn to imitate the cultural model developed and given to them by their dominators. Acceptance of negative self-image promotes political apathy and passivity which in turn results in their withdrawal from political processes. They further develop vague feelings of worry, insecurity and threats and unchallengingly accept the constituted traditional authority (Mussen and Wynzynski, 1952; Freire, 1974).

Economic dependence, constant threat of starvation and the consequent dehumanization create a strong sense of powerlessness and hopelessness among the rural poor. Active involvement of people in development programmes is not possible with such psychological hindrances. It is, therefore, imperative that programmes are directed to remove such negative self-image and the sense of helplessness. Empowerment of people, therefore, becomes an important goal of development, without which efforts for promoting internal capability and productive abilities are not likely to succeed.

8.2. Development of Internal Capability of the People

Developing countries possess vast and rich human resources. The people are intelligent, have sound common sense and are hard-working. Nevertheless, they suffer from illiteracy and their abilities lie dormant. Poor material conditions prevent systematic growth of productive forces, impede improvement of technical skills and retard people's creative capabilities. Social and subjective development and economic development go hand in hand. People from the poor socio-economic class show high political apathy and low feelings of political efficacy and isolation from the mainstream and inaction (Pateman, 1970; Mehta, 1981). Efforts are needed to continually help the poor working people develop their internal resources and capability. This is also important for promoting productive employment.

As mentioned above, planners in India have been emphasizing the importance of promoting organization of the poor. For instance, it was mentioned that it is "necessary for the State machinery to facilitate the process in the initial stages" (Planning Commission, Sixth Plan, 1980 : 4). It has been further noted that success in achieving rapid improvement in the quality of the rural and urban poor will depend upon the extent of involvement of our vast human resources in national development (*ibid*, p. 183).

It is often suggested that a "democratic" system provides scope for everyone to participate and if some people do not do so, it is their fault. Facts are, however, otherwise. People learn to participate by participating and the feelings of political efficacy develop in a participatory environment (Pateman, 1970). Organization of rural workers and their participation in the development process provide them with powerful learning experience, help release their creative abilities and promote social and other skills. Educational and organizational methods are needed to help develop internal capability of the community to enable them to improve their living and working conditions. Promotion of viable and effective organizations of the poor at various levels is, therefore, an important development programme. It is necessary for promoting participation of people for development of their internal capability and for promoting empowerment of the people. It is rather a critical instrument for achieving the objectives of equitable development, as shown by experience in several countries (Szal, 1979).

8.3. Role of Education

The poorest in India are also at the lowest rung of the caste-ridden social hierarchy. They have been suppressed and dominated -- economically and socially -- for centuries. As political parties, trade unions and social activists know from their experience, organizing the poor, particularly the rural poor, is an extremely hazardous and, at times, a volatile task. In the final analysis, the people themselves have to take the initiative. They, however, need support from outside to help them release and strengthen their motivation in this respect. Education can play an important role in this respect.

Participatory Education of the Poor

Educational programmes and training efforts are needed to raise the internal capability of the poor and enhance their skills in promoting and managing their own organizations. Such training cannot obviously be conducted by conventional training and teaching methods.

Development needs suggest certain specific objectives for the education of rural workers. These relate to helping the rural poor develop necessary skills, readiness and motivation for moving toward organizing themselves in various ways and for various purposes. They have necessarily to be related to specific economic, social and human situations. Such "objectives" as discussed in Chapter 6 have been used and tested in a series of educational camps conducted for the rural poor in different parts of the country.

Educational Objectives and Methods

Education of the poor as discussed in Chapter 6 should aim at helping participants develop participatory skills and move from individual to group problem diagnosis. In this process, they learn skills in group work; readiness and skills for problem identification; a sense of collective and "community-ness"; problem-solving approach and action planning. These, in turn, could help them to weaken their dependency syndrome and to enhance a sense of efficacy and a concern for social achievement. Education is thus an integral part of the process of organizing the poor.

The educational methods, therefore, have to be appropriately selected in order to facilitate the above objectives. For example, as discussed in Chapter 6, the participants could be involved in exercises, games, small group discussions and in a(planning. Efforts should be directed to help them internali. .onceptual diagnosis of their problems and to develop readiness for problem solving and asserting. The content and methods of training and the learning process, therefore, need to be directed to enhance their skills and a sense of efficacy, and towards their psychological empowerment.

8.4. Some Experience Based Insights Relevant for Organizing

Facilitating and Hindering Forces

Training cannot be separated from the work of organizing and empowerment of the poor. These are intimately inter-related. Experience reports of many developing countries including India are now available, which document the process of empowering and organizing the rural poor (Huizer, 1972; Rahman, 1983; Huizer, 1973; Chandra and Mehta, 1984, ILO, 1986). Such experience reports suggest valuable insights, like the following, which could facilitate the tasks of promoting effective organizations.

Rural Poor have a Strong Desire to Learn

They expect outsiders to teach them. Experience of working with the poor suggests three important things which an organizer needs to do for the poor peasants. First, he is to live exactly as they do. Secondly, he is to talk with them about the land which used to belong to them in their grandfathers' days. Thirdly, he "must always be teaching them something. I am not an intellectual so I teach them football, but learn they must. They insist on it". (Huizer, 1972 : 42). It implies that the organizer should live among the rural poor, otherwise he cannot teach them and/or inspire confidence among them and stand by them in times of their need.

Poor Live in a World of Fear

As is well known, the rural poor including the tribal poor live in a world of fear. For instance, they fear the rent collector, they fear the policeman, they fear anyone who looks like an official and thus who claims authority for them. They fear the moneylender and his patrons. They fear evil spirits who threaten their children and their cattle. They even fear the strength of their neighbour. In such a situation, no wonder, their xenophobia includes officials, man in bush-shirt and trousers, men who come on bicycles and jeeps but never on their feet, and who by the very definition come with some hidden traps (Bailey, 1973 : 300-303). Such fears tend to promote negative self-image, as mentioned above, and reinforce their sense of helplessness and powerlessness.

Rumours Spread Quickly in Villages

Combined with the all-prevading sense of fear is the power of rumours. They spread like wildfire among the village poor. For instance, at the beginning of the participatory project in Singari (Chandra and Mehta, 1984), a strong rumour spread among the villagers that government officials were going there to evict them from their land. They mistook the organizer himself as such an official. They were, therefore, instantly alerted against the organizer. The village people tend to view the presence of outsiders with suspicion. The trust about which we often talk in the context of organizations is shrouded under in-built suspicions and fears among the rural poor. Such a mistrust cannot be removed by mere physical presence or by talking.

Credibility of Government Institutions

It is ironical that the village poor look to any government official or anybody connected with any government institution with suspicion. Many a time even the organizers who go there to help them are also looked upon as government officials. Because of their past experience, credibility of such institutions is generally low among the villagers. This factor always comes in the way when outsiders go to villages for organizing the poor.

8.5. Interventions for Promoting Organization of Rural Poor

The rural poor need outside help for starting the process of organizing themselves. The help-seeking and help-giving process has to take place in the socio-psychological context briefly outlined above. Interventions, therefore, have to be designed in order to establish initial rapport with the village poor including the tribal poor. For instance, in the experimental project mentioned above and briefly discussed in Chapter 9, initial communication was established through a night discussion-group participated by some of the village youth. They were provided with lighting facility and reading and writing materials. Gradually, some local youth were persuaded to work as part-time teachers at a night literacy class.

The response was not at all encouraging. Absence of education among them, reluctance to leave their hamlets, need to spend time with their family members, fear of darkness, dangerous animals and reptiles as well as physical presence of several educated unemployed in the village discouraged them from attending night classes. Above all, there was the lurking mistrust about the intentions of the organizers of the night classes. Their skepticism and mistrust continued unabated for several months. Only five to six persons used to come and the attendance did not improve. Under such conditions, literacy classes suffered from the same problems as has been repeatedly documented in respect of similar adult education programmes (Mehta, 1990). The people did not see any value in such education. They also did not trust the organizers. Under such conditions, it was difficult to talk of organizing as well as of education. The main task, therefore, was to win the confidence of the people.

One such opportunity came when it was reported, and quickly and widely circulated among the villagers, that one of them was forced to pay rather a heavy bribe to one of the policemen. This was not very unusual for the village people and there was nothing new in it. However, what was new was their visible resentment. The very fact that the event became a subject matter of whispers was important. Organizers seized this opportunity and brought up this issue at the night class. Slowly, discussions hotted up. At such a stage, the organizer suggested that the police could be forced to give back the bribe money. As could be expected, the people would not believe it. The same group of the night class learners, however, thought that it was time to test the credentials of the group organizers. There was nothing wrong in trying. Hence came the first major confrontation with the police. Fortunately in this case, the project personnel were able to persuade some top bureaucrats in the district to come to their help. With their intervention, the policemen was forced to return the bribe money in broad daylight in the market and in the presence of many other villagers. Thus, the individual event became a group learning experience. This success experience considerably improved the people's confidence in the project personnel. As a result, they started throging the night class. This experience significantly accelerated the organizing as well as the educational process. Soon, the night school became the community centre of the village. The village poor started realizing the utility of education. It was interesting to observe the psychological change. The poor illiterate and sceptical people started "demanding" education. And the night school space became too small to accommodate the increasing numbers.

Voluntary Prohibition

In this particular case, it was a tribal village where the project personnel were trying to promote education and organization of the poor. After the initial experience of success with the policeman, the group organizers brought together some youth to discuss the pressing problems of the village. They brought up the need for voluntary prohibition in the village as their topmost priority. The youth were sensitive to the problems created by excessive drinking in the village. Half a dozen young men, there and then, volunteered to give up drinking. These young men later convened a larger meeting to discuss the problems of drinking. They were acutely aware of the evil, but were waiting for a determined leadership. The meeting resolved to have their own prohibition in the village. They, now, saw the need for an organization so that prohibition could be effectively enforced. Thus, the *Village Council*—their own organization—was born.

Confronting Money-lenders

The self-imposed prohibition was a very good success. This was unique in view of the fact that drinking among the tribals is a common and strong habit. With this success, the ill effects of drinking gradually started disappearing from the village. Such positive experience later motivated them to confront the village money-lenders. The executive committee of the Village Council decided that nobody would pay anything to money-lenders and that those found paying would be severely dealt with by the organization. Thereafter, a large meeting of the community was convened where a detailed account was taken as to who had borrowed how much money and how much had been refunded to the money-lender. The information thus collected was rather a shock to everyone. They had already returned much more than what they had borrowed to the money-lenders. At this moment, the decision of the Executive Council was placed before the entire general body of the people. There was a heated discussion for several hours. There were fears, apprehensions and scepticism. After through discussions, the general body of the villagers confirmed the decision of the Executive Committee that nobody would pay any longer to the money-lenders. In order to meet the contingencies, it was further decided to set up some grain-cum-cash "bank" as a necessary borrowing facility on a nominal interest. The village organization itself would handle this "bank".

As was expected, the moneylenders did not take the decision lightly. They started pressuring and intimidating the village people. They tried to create disunity and disaffection amongst them. One of the money-lenders even threatened one particular villager that he would be killed if he did not behave. The matter was again brought up in the Village Council. The village community came together and exhibited courage and cohesiveness. They decided to alert the police to take necessary steps to avoid any trouble. These decisions, taken collectively by the Village Council, worked as law for the people. The moneylenders also gradually realized this and dared not start any trouble.

Encouraged by the initial success, the Village Council planned and implemented several important socio-economic projects. For instance, the Council launched an educational campaign against the practice of litigation and helped the people to settle their disputes themselves. They also undertook several new economic projects with the help of the district administration. These projects resulted in a substantial increase in their income as well as savings. The income-generating projects gave them further confidence, reinforced their sense of efficacy and strengthened their faith in the organization. But with success came internal conflicts. As discussed in Chapter 9, with their newfound awareness, confidence, assertion and skills, they were able to tackle their internal problems. They were able to convert their mistakes and failures into learning experience.

8.6. Some Conceptual Issues

It is not intended here to generalize from just one project. However, the experience did provide some valuable conceptual and practical lessons on educating, organizing and empowering the poor. It was clear, for example, that the group organizer played a vital and critical role in stimulating and accelerating the process of forming organizations. In this respect, the personal qualities and skills of the group organizer were themselves a critical resource. It was possible to seek and get help from committed and honest bureaucrats not only to contain the atrocities of the police and moneylenders but also in sustaining the organization through several socio-economic projects. It was also, however, found that such committed officials were likely to be transferred away from the project, even when the project needed them, hence the all-important need for inculcation of their own internal capability. The dependency syndrone of the poor required concrete interventions and vigilance on their own part. They needed to develop an alternative credit facility and security system of their own.

One of the important lessons was the need for shared and collective leadership. Such leadership was needed so that no one single individual could dominate the scene. Collective efforts were very important in this respect which alone could sustain the organization and cement unity of the poor against corruption and other illegal practices.

Psychological Development

Research reveals that, citizens learn a sense of political efficacy under certain socio-economic conditions. Persons having greater opportunity of participation at work and other places, and greater exposure to education, even literacy, are likely to have a greater sense of efficacy. Such research findings as well as practical experience have immense implications for development theory and strategies. Organizations of the poor and participatory development promote development of people : enhance their sense of efficacy and assertion and psychological development in various ways.

Their shyness is broken. Their vague fears and cynicism begin to melt away. Their articulation returns and they begin to speak out—loud and clear. They acquire new consciousness for settling their disputes and wasteful litigations are given up. Their creativity is released and they are able to design and implement several innovative socio-economic projects. Their appetite for education is aroused and they are ready to learn more and more. The natural militancy among women gets channelized and they become active partners in this process of education and development. The organization and their active participation bring to the people several important educational and developmental gains. Some such details are discussed in Chapter 9.

9

PARTICIPATION, EDUCATION AND HUMAN DEVELOPMENT

A CITIZEN'S feeling that he was competent to follow the functioning of government, politics and civic activities, that he could influence them and that he could get things done with the help of the elected representatives and government officials indicate his sense o subjective competence in relation to the socio-economic and political process. Such a psychological resource was a significant facilitating factor in the people's efforts for organization, as discussed in Chapter 7. Such a sense of competence releases energy for concerted action. As discussed in Chapter 5, thoughts and feelings of being competent and capable of influencing, environment weakens the traditional negative self-concept and dependency behaviour. Sense of efficacy, thus, forms an important human resource.

Low Efficacy Among the Poor

Socio-economically weaker sections of our population have been as is well known, low on sense of political efficacy as compared to better-off sections. This has been documented by several studies (Arora, 1969; Roy, 1975; Atal, 1969). It is no surprise, as the poorer people, particularly the rural poor, have long been isolated from the mainstream of the society and the polity. The long period during which politics in India remained the prerogative of alien rulers further confirmed the image of politics and government as far removed from the day-to-day mores and folk ways. The national movement sought to bring the masses into the mainstream of the socio-political struggle for independence. Various activities since independence, particularly elections and democratic institutions, have helped this process of inclusion.

Development and Widening Gap between Rich and Poor

Development programmes do not necessarily help the poor, particularly the rural poor. Despite such development, as discussed in the preceding chapters, the gap between the rich and the poor has tended to widen in the developing countries. In the absence of participation and assertion, people are not able to obtain fruits of development. They not only become economically poorer but also psychologically more powerless (FAO, 1980). Their sense of powerlessness further prevents them from taking advantage of their entitlements and development opportunities.

Efficacy, Education and Participation

Education has repeatedly shown significant relationship with citizen's sense of political efficacy. Even a little movement from total illiteracy to literacy shows a significant increase in the sense of political efficacy (Mehta, 1981). Participation in election campaigns also emerges as a significant factor (Ahmed, 1971). Workers' participation in trade unions promotes political consciousness and efficacy in them (Ashraf, 1975). Cross-cultural studies in several countries show that, the individual, who has consistent opportunities for non-political participation, such as in decisions at the place of work, develops a sense of political efficacy. He is move likely to generate this to greater political participation in order to influence national and local government decisions. (Almond and Verba, 1963 : 363-66).

9.1. People's Self–Action for Development

An opportunity came to test the hypothesis regarding participation and psychological development of people during an experimental development project. As mentioned in Chapter 8, this project, involving a very backward tribal community in a remote village, was based on participatory education and organization of the village poor. It was the people's self-action for development where they initiated, planned, executed and monitored several programmes. As described earlier, the village people organized themselves into a Village Council (named as *Chotanagpur Gram Karandar Samiti*) and launched upon a modest programme of socio-economic development. They were able to achieve several social as well as economic gains.

Village Profile when Project was Launched

As the participatory project continued for some time, the people gained confidence. They started perceiving a change in their lives and their thinking. The President and the Secretary of the Village Council then jointly recalled and prepared a self-report about the picture of the socio-economic conditions of the village at the time when the development programme was launched. The project was initiated in early 1979. The self-report was prepared in October, 1982. It was prepared in Nagpuria, a local tribal dialect, and written by the village leaders in their own hand. It contains vivid descriptions in rich and cogent local idiom. The force of their feelings has somewhat been lost in translation. However, the following are some relevant excerpts :

> "People used to steal small things from each other. For any fault, big or small, the village chiefs (Mehtos) and chowkidars would award monetary punishment. The amount thus collected would be mostly spent on drinking and fuddling, in which the village people took an active part, taking a holiday from all domestic/agricultural activities. This would invariably result in a great loss. Some of them in their drunken fits would throw their children out of the house. Then, somebody, knowing that the fellow was not in his senses, would swindle him of everything."
>
> "There was a school teacher in the village but there was no school building. Nobody bothered whether the children went to school or whether the teacher taught them. Some ten children used to go to school. Nobody even cared whether they had any reading or writing material or whether they were clean or even dressed. There was no fixed time for sending them to school. Education was considered a casual affair, as children could earn by working somewhere."
>
> "The primary thing was that the domestic work should be carried out and education did not make much sense. The people used to ask if children did not run errands at home, would they become Sahibs (Officers) after education?"
>
> "Any official, whether a sepoy or a peon, used to walk into the village, lay himself cosily on a charpoy and order us to arrange for his feasting of rice and chicken. The villagers, being ignorant and scared, would not protest. They would

arrange whatever the officials demanded. Except for the Block Development Office (BDO) at Angara, the nearby Block, they had not seen any government office. They dared not enter the BDO's office, nor venture to write an application. This was due to fear, hesitation and drinking." "They lost their land to money-lenders and traders in the process of drinking. The amount to be paid back mounted year after year. Neither the people left drinking, nor the money-lenders left coming to them. If the people failed to pay any instalment, the moneylenders would confiscate all their belongings – animate and inanimate."

Low Efficacy and Assertion

It was thus clear that the villagers' self-esteem and sense of efficacy and assertion were very low, as could be expected. It was interesting that the village leaders were able to recall the picture so vividly. The self-reports indicated the villagers' robust commonsense, a sense of humour and an insight into the nature of their problems.

Participatory Development Process

The development project was launched with a series of educational interventions. The village people gradually organized themselves into a Village Council with paid membership and elected office-bearers. Under the leadership of the Council, the people initiated a number of socio-economic projects. They took decisions, educated others about such decisions, and vigorously implemented such programmes. Some details regarding the process, inputs and results of the projects have been described in Chapter 8.

9.2. Behavioural Indicators of Emerging Efficacy and Assertion

The people gradually gained confidence in their capacity for self-action. Efforts for organizing themselves were the most important step in this direction. The village people could perceive the changes taking place in their mental outlook and self-esteem. The President and the Secretary of the Village Council prepared various self-reports about these changes as they perceived them.

One sample from their self-reports has been mentioned above. The following interesting points emerged from such reports and from the research findings.

Enhanced Morale and Education

As already mentioned in Chapter 8, the very first decision the people took after taking the initiative in their own hands, was to stop drinking altogether. This had a salutary effect on their morale. This also resulted in considerable savings, which enabled them to take risk and plan new socio-economic activities. Through a process of struggle and awareness, they were awakened to the need for education of their children and for themselves. They constructed a school for their children, set up several night classes for adults – both male and female – and appointed teachers and instructors from their own funds. As a result, there was a tremendous upsurge in adult literacy and in the children's school-going tendency.

Interface with Officials : Emerging Sense of Assertion

Their changing consciousness was also reflected in their attitude to the officials. Like other rural poor, the people at Singari were also traditionally afraid of officials. They dared not open their mouth and talk to them about their hardships. The question of registering any kind of protest did not arise. In fact, most of them had hardly seen a government office or an officer. The self-action projects, however, changed this very significantly for the Singari people. In pursuit of project activities and the activities of the Village Council, the office-bearers and ordinary members of the Council went to various government offices at the Block and higher levels. Initially, they were accompanied by a social worker – the resident coordinator of the project. However, they soon learnt to meet the officials on their own. As the President of the Village Council put it, "now we can talk on our matters with any officer without anybody's help and can get things done on our own."

Their suppressed desire for taking things in their own hands was awakened. Success experience further reinforced their sense of assertion. The project soon attracted the attention of the officials who now visited the village more frequently. During one such visit, the villagers talked to one senior official about lack of irrigation in the village. Fortunately for them, this official was helpful. Very soon they got government aid for digging new wells and for repairing the old ones. This was one among several other examples, where additional resources were obtained with their own initiative and insight. This greatly helped their various socio-economic projects. They could relate such success with their own efforts which boosted their need for achievement and concern for quality of life.

Problem Solving Approach

As illustrated by the above examples, the village people were not afraid of taking risks. Nor did they run away from problems. They now showed a problem-solving approach. In this process, they learnt to "manage" help from various developmental agencies. They also confronted their own social problems like drinking and wasteful expenditure on marriages and other social occasions. They did not just pass resolutions at the Council meetings but established a mechanism for enforcing norms against drinking and wasteful expenditure. They showed the same activist approach to providing education for their children and for themselves. In yet another instance, they were confronted with supply of rotton cattle feed by some outside firm. They went up to the highest officials and got it replaced with better quality feed. They did not just complain but took collective action to solve their day-to-day problems.

It is interesting, as reported earlier by the village people themselves, that under the influence of liquor and indebtedness, the village people became rather docile, wasted their time and did nothing, except indulging in more and more drinking and in borrowing money. In a way, alcoholic habits were the manifestation of their fears and powerlessness. As they participated in developmental activities, both objective and subjective factors started changing. They were encouraged by the positive results of their efforts. They became actors in the process of development. In a way, they were changed people with an increasing sense of self-esteem, a sense of hope and assertion.

Confronting Corrupt Elected Office-bearers

The emerging skills for confronting social and economic problems and their enhanced sense of efficacy were reflected remarkably during the latter part of the development project in a rather unique way. One of the main office-bearers of the Village Council, its Secretary, who was leading them for quite some-time since the beginning of the project, was strongly confronted by the village people. The Village Council had earlier got a fair price shop in the village which they entrusted to the care of their Secretary. Unfortunately, this office-bearer was corrupted. The President of the Village Council put it so succinctly. He reported, "Considering us ignorant, he became proud and selfish and started ignoring the opinion of the people. He even started cheating in weight at the fair price shop. The weight of every article he weighed was about five grams less per kilo but the price charged was for full one kilo."

The village people brought these issues to the Village Council. It was further reported that "when we raised these matters in the meetings of the Village Council, for a month or so, being uppish, he hotly refused to amend his mistakes". Eventually, this person refused to attend the meetings of the Council. Instead he contacted the police and went against the interest of the village. This resulted in a direct confrontation between the village people and the police. During this period of confrontation, and later, the village people remained united. They succeeded in removing the corrupt office-bearer from his post. They elected a new person as the Secretary of the Village Council. The earlier Secretary was socially bycotted. This eventually brought him back to his senses and he repented his conduct.

9.3. Enhanced Sense of Efficacy and Assertion for Social Development

The above instances provided continuing evidence of an increasing sense of efficacy and assertion among the village people. They could initiate several actions on their own. They learnt to confront problems and officials. They learnt to seek help and manage their organization and other activities with satisfying results. They were no longer the drunken, docile, timid and servile people. They were emerging as actors. They now thought that their actions would make a difference and they could influence men and matters, including the officials.

Performance Consciousness

Towards the end of the project, some structured interviews were conducted with a small group of villagers, both men and women. Responding to various questions, the village people talked about various aspects of the project including changes which they perceived as a result of the project. They showed a high degree of awareness about the various project inputs and activities and recalled various gains obtained in the project.

The availability of gains did not make them complacent as indicated by their suggested need for improvement in the project. Thus, 80 per cent of the respondents thought that there was a need for further improvement in the project. Asked to specify, they gave various suggestions. Some one-third of them thought, more help was required in their various activities. One in every five respondents perceived the need for greater unity and strong organization, involving women in all such efforts. Many of them suggested establishment of cottage industry and enhancement of irrigation in the village. The suggested action for improvement underlined their concern for good performance, a sense of vigilance and awareness about the functioning of the project and a need for social achievement. They were specific about various activity goals which again showed their concern for social achievement (Mehta, 1982, 1994).

Aspirations for Children (Boys)

The value of education was further highlighted by the projected aspirations of the parents for their children (boys). Some 90 per cent of the respondents were in favour of giving higher education to their children. When probed, they were able to specify their aspirations. For instance, one-third of them wanted their children to become teachers. One in every 10 wanted them to become BDOs (Block Development Officers, who are important government functionaries for development). Some others wanted their children to become Gram Sevaks (village level workers), technicians, social workers, doctors and bank managers. It was interesting to find that the respondents thought of jobs of such persons with whom they had come in contact. The expressed aspirations clearly indicated their perceived importance of education as well as a sense of upward mobility for their children.

Aspirations for Children (Girls) : Changing Concept of Women

The respondents were equally in favour of education of the girls. Some 8 to 9 out of every 10 of them wished to give education to their daughters. They thought that education would make them wise, prepare them for service to the community and help them conduct their business properly. Several of them thought that education would prepare them for a better domestic life. They also thought that education was essential for development. Given the traditional context of our rural people, particularly tribals, parents' aspirations for daughters assumed great importance. It also showed their changing self-concept as well as their concept of women.

Hope of Better Life for Children

The people were not only in favour of education including higher education of both boys and girls, and, they not only aspired for better work for them; most remarkably, they were quite hopeful of achieving such aspirations. Thus, some 87 per cent of them, *i.e.* 8 to 9 respondents out of every 10, hoped to achieve such goals. Such hope of success was noteworthy in people traditionally known for cynicism for development. In a way, it revealed the vibrant and optimistic nature of the tribal people. Here, such hope was associated with development goals, and with self-action.

Social Development

One of the major and early outcomes of the self-action project in the village was self-imposed enforcement of prohibition. When asked about this situation, some 8 to 9 out of every 10 reported to have left drinking. Only one of them (i.e. 10 per cent) was still drinking. All of them reported that they had give up drinking in pursuance of the new norms developed and enforced by the Village Council. That the enforcement of prohibition was not coercive but really voluntary, was revealed when nearly two-thirds of them recalled that thereafter there were no quarrels in the village. Some 8 out of every 10 thought that it meant considerable saving for them. They were happy as there was greater harmony in the family. It was clear that the people genuinely thought that the voluntary prohibition was very useful and highly desirable.

Organization of Village Council

One of the outstanding achievements of the development project was the establishment of an organization, namely, the Village Council. Each one of the respondents was aware of the organization in the village. They knew the time and the manner in which such a Village Council was formed. They knew about the last elections in the Village Council. Such responses indicated that the Village Council – their organization for self-action – had gone deep into thinking and was a living reality in their life.

Functions of the Village Council

They thought of the Council as their leader and guide. For instance, they recalled that it arranged loans for them from time to time; helped them in resolving conflicts and quarrels; united the people and helped the poor when in need; taught them the right way of cultivation; arranged education for them and their children, etc. Their awareness of the organization was, therefore, not just nominal. It was clear that their image of the Village Council was deep and real with a clear perception of the activities and functions of the Council. Interestingly, practically every one of them reported that they were participating in the Village Council and in its meetings. Probed further, two-thirds of them were participating as members and one in every 10 respondents was an office-bearer and the remaining were participating as villagers. Every one of them thought that the Village Council was serving a useful purpose and that it was essential for them.

Health Care

One of the recurring problems faced by the village community is the non-availability of medical treatment and health facilities. There was supposed to be a health centre in the village which was, however, not functioning. When asked what kind of treatment they provide when somebody fell sick in the family, a large majority of the respondents reported to be using the services of a witch-doctor. They were also using some locally available herbs. Only few of them reported that they took their sick to a health centre or to a doctor. The nearest health centre was located some 11 km away from the village without a proper road. No transport was available to the village people. They were, therefore, forced to carry the sick to the health centre physically on their shoulders in case they wanted to consult the doctor there. It was too much of a hardship. The witch-doctor was readily available in the village. Out of sheer lack of facilities, they were forced to take the services of such a quack. This was antithetic to their emerging "modernity". They were keen to have a functioning health centre in their own village.

9.4. People's Subjective Development

Women's Changing Self-concept

The Singari women had registered a tremendous gain in literacy, as discussed earlier. This was indicative of positive subjective changes in them. A small group of women were also interviewed to obtain some relevant date. Some such findings are discussed below :

Desire for Education

Most of the women interviewed for the study were aware of the day school as well as of the night school. However, only 4 out of every 10 respondents were actually attending school. When asked for reasons for this, one-third of them said they could not because of the infant children at home. Two of them were too old to go to school and one did not have sufficient time. It was interesting to find that lack of time was not perceived as so important a factor in this connection. It was probably young mothers with infants who could not go. Each one of them saw the importance of the night school. They thought that women should learn to read and write because it would make them wise; they would be able to read and write letters and do other work. All of them were satisfied with the night schools. It was noteworthy that each one of the eligible mothers was in favour of education for their children in the day school. They also favoured higher education for their children.

Aspirations for Children

The young females were not only in favour of giving higher education to their children but they had specific aspersions for them.

For example, they wished that their children become teachers, government officials and skilled workers. Almost every one of them was hopeful to achieve such aspirations for their children.

Girls' Education

All of them were also in favour of giving education to girls. They thought that education would help them perform their domestic work in a better way; they would be able to read and write and would be able to talk to anyone without hesitation. They also thought that education would make them wise.

More Time for Family

Practically, all the women were working in the village. Before the project was launched, 4 out of every 10 women interviewed worked outside the village. The project activities had enabled them to work in the village itself. Due to this change, they thought they were able to devote more time to their family and take care of children. At the same time it enabled them to have sufficient time to look after their fields and do other work at home and outside.

Health Care

It was interesting here to know that one-third to one-half of the female respondents preferred to take their sick to a private doctor. However, others preferred to go to a witch-doctor and to use local herbs. This was an interesting difference with men where most of them preferred to use the local witch-doctor instead of bothering to go to a doctor. They were probably opting for an easy way out. In this sense, females showed a better appreciation of proper health care.

9.5. Development of Psychological Modernity : Men's Changing Behaviour

Conceptually, it was hypothesized that the people's participation in development projects and participatory education would promote their subjective development. They would not only develop positive self-concept but would also show a sense of upward mobility. Their general approach and attitudes would become psychologically more "modern". Date were obtained on some aspects of such subjective modernity. The behaviour of men and women is discussed separately, for, the letter's attitudes have an additional importance.

Change in Old Ways of Cultivation

All but two male respondents, i.e. 28 out of 30 persons interviewed, favoured changes in the old methods and ways of cultivation in order to increase production. Only two of them thought that introduction of new methods would be a sheer waste of time and that they should continue with the old methods. Thus, an overwhelming number of the village people appreciated the need and importance of change in the agricultural methods suggesting modernity in their thinking.

Qualifications for High Office

When asked about the Qualifications and other requirements necessary for persons holding a high office, almost three-fourths of them perceived higher education and special knowledge as the basis for such an office and the remaining one-fourth, interestingly, favoured popularity with people as the condition for holding such an office. It was remarkable that none of them thought of family connections and traditional roles in this regard.

Future of the Country

Expressing their opinion about the factors responsible for a better future of the country, more than 90 per cent perceived hard labour of the people as the most important factor in this connection. Only one out of 30 thought that it would depend on the grace of God and another one thought good luck as an important factor in this connection. Again, it was remarkable that the tribal respondents were quite clear about the need and importance of hard work for success and development.

Family Planning Acceptable

Their emerging modernity was further revealed by their attitude to controlling the size of family. As many as 9 out of 10 favoured family planning for limiting the number of children so that the parents could look after them properly. The remaining 10, i.e. only 10 per cent, thought that it was wrong to deliberately limit the size of family and stop children.

Appreciation of Events

Practically every one of them was interested in knowing about the events in their village, their neighourhood and about agriculture. They were interested in getting such information. World affairs, events at the national level, religious functions, etc., did not attract even one of them. Such items were not news worthy for them.

Relating to Visitors from Abroad and Distant Lands

Would they appreciate the ways and lifestyles of visitors from other countries and would they like an opportunity of meeting such persons? More than 50 per cent of them thought, they would like such meetings and would be glad to know about their ways of living. Nearly one-fourth of them did not have any views. Here again it was remarkable that persons living in a remote village practically cut off from the outside world were not hesitant to meet strangers form abroad, to talk to them and to appreciate their ways of living. Here it may be mentioned that some of the respondents had come in contact with foreigners coming to study the project in the village. This was in such a contrast with their traditional mistrust of outsiders. They were no longer suspicious and afraid of them.

Membership and Knowledge about Organizations

When asked about their relationship with any organization, most of them – about 90 per cent – readily recalled the organization of the Village Council – the Gram Sabha. They belonged to this Gram Sabha. It was also interesting that they did not name nay other organization or some political party or a religious group. It was obvious that they were keenly interested in the Village Council and felt a sense of belonging to it.

9.6. Psychological Modernity in Women

The same data, as discussed for men above, were also obtained from women. It was remarkable that Singari women showed a sense of modernity. For instance, all of them favoured introduction of new methods of cultivation for increasing production. None of them had any doubt in this regard. An overwhelming number of them favoured qualifications like education, special knowledge and skills and popularity with the people as the basis for appointment to a high office. Here also none of them thought of caste and other such traditional considerations. A large number of them considered their own hard work as the most important factor in the progress of the country. They also considered good planning on part of the government as an important factor in this regard. Interestingly, none of hem thought of good luck and grace of God as the factors in this regard. Many of hem were also keen to know about the local events. Most of them were in favour of meeting and knowing about foreigners and appreciated different ways of living. One in every two women interviewed distinctly recalled the Village Council and its activities. They were members of this organization. A large number of them recalled lack of proper market and proper irrigation facilities as their important problems.

It was clear that the women had undergone a significant learning process. It was such a contrast from women in general living in remote backward areas. It was obvious that they considered themselves as active partners in development activities, particularly those initiated in their village. The spread-over of social learning was remarkable as changes had occurred also in areas in which the project did not make any direct input such as family planning. The findings underlined the importance of participatory education and social learning in moulding the people's self-concept which in turn becomes a factor in socio-economic development. That, village women showed a significant change in their self-concept and in their thinking was in itself an important achievement of the project.

Overall Modernity

The data clearly showed substantial gains in the sense of overall modernity—both in men and more importantly in women in the village. Such changes were indeed very significant in view of the earlier documentation that these occurred mostly in persons exposed to factory work and in urban life (Inkeles and Smith, 1974). The village was initially very backward with very low literacy among men and nil among women. They were suspicious of the outside world. They viewed them only as exploiters, though not very wrongly. Lack of transport and means of communication and lack of other infrastructure was a big problem. However, the mentality of the village and of the people had changed positively. This was also more remarkable as such changes had occurred among sections of the most backward of the tribal community, namely, the Bedias in Bihar. The people had achieved a high degree of change proneness; sense of personal efficacy; appreciation of skills and education; appreciation of hard work as a factor in achievement; appreciation for population control and, above all, appreciation of the importance of an effective organization. Such behavioural changes in women were more significant and important for further socio-economic changes.

9.7. Promoting Human Development

Objective and Subjective Factors

There was, thus, a continuous interaction between and among objective and subjective factors resulting in socio-economic changes in the village. Some such factors are seen in Fig. 9.1. The people's action for development, that is, participatory development, contributed to people's organizations and in development of at least some infrastructure in the form of irrigation, schools, bank credit and new economic projects. There were significant gains in employment and work resulting in additional income for the household. The people were motivated to actively participate in various activities of the organization, i.e. the Village Council, and in various other projects initiated by them.

Success in such projects reinforced and strengthened social learning of a new self-concept and further motivated them to actively participate in various projects and affairs of their community. Such participation was a remarkable and new learning experience for them. It greatly contributed to their education and to releasing their productive and creative energy. They were able to

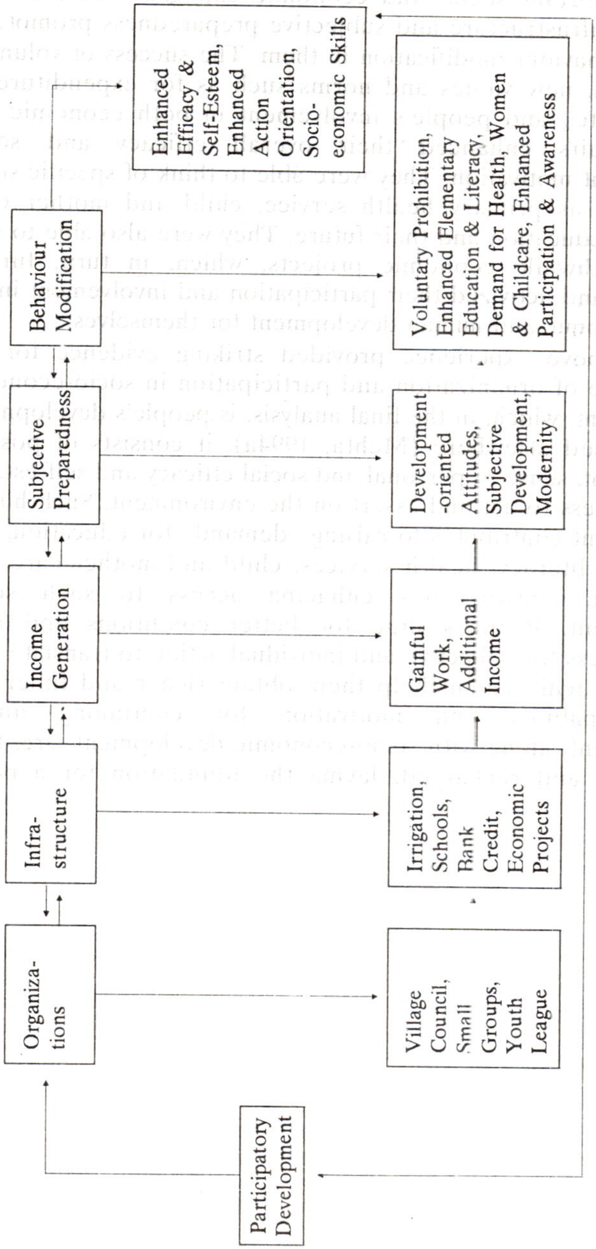

FIG. 9.1 : Objective and Subjective Factors in Human Development

obtain important social and economic changes. Interaction of objective infrastructure and subjective preparedness promoted a positive behaviour modification in them. The success of voluntary prohibition, new values and norms such as for expenditure on festivals, etc., and people's involvement in both economic and social affairs enhanced their overall efficacy and social achievement motivation. They were able to think of specific social goals such as primary health service, child and mother care, children's education and their future. They were also able to plan some worthwhile economic projects, which, in turn, further enhanced and activized their participation and involvement in the socio-economic and human development for themselves.

The above experience provided striking evidence for the importance of organization and participation in socio-economic development, which, in the final analysis, is people's development. As discussed elsewhere (Mehta, 1994a), it consists of positive self-concept, sense of personal and social efficacy and self-esteem, and readiness to act and assert on the environment. Such human development contributes to raising "demand" for education, skill formation, literacy, health services, child and mother care, and population control, thus enhacing access to such social development. People's urge for better conditions and their preparedness for collective and individual action to translate such goals into achievement help them obtain richer and fuller life. Their capability and motivation for continuing human development, along with socio-economic development, are, thus, reinforced and recharged, laying the foundation for a better society.

APPENDICES

APPENDIX-I

SOME SELF-REPORTS ON SOCIO-ECONOMIC CONDITIONS*

Specimens from Banswara Camp (July 27 – August 1, 1978)

1. *Haldhar* (Kushalganj Tehsil) : There is no house. We cannot get wood from the forest. They do not give free pass. Farmers have been given land but no allotment. At many places the Forest Department has taken over the land and, therefore, we are landless. There is no drinking water facility. We have to bring water from a long distance.

We need a tank for water, a hostel for our children and some small industries for work. There are collective accounts for land. We want an individual account for each piece of land. Some families have been selected for the Antyodaya Programme, but they have not received any land yet.

In the settlement, land has gone under demarcation. We have to pay a penalty for using it for farming. They have confiscated the land for plantation. We are beaten up by them. The forest people are very cruel to us. They do not even allow us to use the land for our cattle. They are themselves destroying forest and at the same time taking away our land for plantation.

2. *Udai Singh* : Generally Harijan families have many children and no land. A few of them may have one to two acres. They earn about Rs. 3 a day and have to spend more than this. To get work for one day we have to wait and sit at home for two days. Children go to school without proper clothes and the teacher throws them out from the class. There are boys with education up to VIII to X class, but have no work.

* Translated from the original text written/spoken in Hindi mixed with the local dialect.

We have neither bamboo nor wood for our huts. One bamboo costs Rs. 8 and we may make three baskets from one bamboo. It is, therefore, not at all paying.

Nobody listens to us, neither the minister, nor the *Sarpanch* nor the *Patwari*.

3. *Baldev* (Kankarbari, Kurbalghar Tehsil) : In Banswara, 90 per cent people are tribals and Harijans. Out of 120 houses in our village only four families have land. The rest of them have to do *majduri* (labour) getting Rs. 2 to 2.50 for a day for males and Rs. 2 and even less than this for females. There are no fixed rates. We have to steal wood from the forest in order to survive. Most houses are made of wood and bamboo which are now in a very bad condition. They can be completely washed away by rains. This is the condition of the entire area. It is a hilly area. There is no facility for irrigation. The people of the tehsil are always in trouble, sometimes due to floods and sometimes due to drought. There is no fixed work. The relief work is for 15 days in a month. In rest of the days, there is no work. There is no facility for transport. We do not get any seed or fertilizer. The Cooperative Stores sell these to the traders, who charge Rs. 105 for one bag of fertilizer, whereas they pay only Rs. 85 to the Store. The relief work gives Rs. 12 in a week. This is given on the basis of *napti*, i.e. digging of pit measuring 10′ by 12′. Five persons dig one pit a day. Some people working on the tar roads get 15 days' wage and about 20 kg. of wheat per month.

He is educated up to class X and is working on a farm.

4. *Kalla* (Parten) : We do not get our wages on time. We have to go from place to place for work.

5. *Kanhyalal* (Bagidora Tehsil) : Most people are tribals and Harijans in the Tehsil. Most of us are engaged in farming. The government does not provide us with necessary means and facilities for farming. Due to poverty, people are not able to purchase seed, bullocks, etc. We do not get loans. We have to give fees (bribe) for everything including education, for getting admission to schools. Not even 25 per cent have regular work. Officials spoil all for us.

6. *Mansukh* : He makes bamboo baskets. One bamboo costs about Rs. 7. Three to four baskets can be made out of one bamboo. One bamboo fetches 2 *paili* grain, about Rs. 2.50. We have nothing – neither a house, nor a cow, nor a bullock – just nothing. The daily wage is between Rs. 2 and 2.50.

7. *Codara Dhana* (Bagidora Tehsil) : I have been selected in Antyodaya and given 5.75 bigha of land. Other three persons have been given 3 acres each. Another person have been given Rs. 400 as aid. Others have not got any aid. Land is very bad. We are unable to farm it.

8. *Bala Ram* (Bagidora Tehsil) : Some people have five to six acres. There are no means of irrigation. People do not have any income; therefore, they live on debts. That is why the *sagri* system comes. They are having social evils and indulge in wrong activities. The moneylenders force them into wrong things and then they are forced to take loans from them. Persons in the village are born in debt, live in debt and die in debt. Houses are of bamboo and wood. Harijans suffer from many diseases. The barbers do not cut their hair. If they do so they charge more money. They are given *sagri* by the farmers, i.e. grain for one year in lieu of wages.

The village itself is responsible for its difficulties. There are so many government rules, but implementation is not there. The scheme for giving loans is just nothing. Two years ago I filled a form for getting a loan. I had to go twice to the town for this purpose and spent Rs. 200 in the process. The loan has still not come.

9. *Bansala Gaon* (Bagidora Tehsil) : In my village nobody drinks. The caste *Niat* (Council) has stopped it. Our houses are very weak. Our farm land is broken. There is a need for a boundary wall. We also need bullocks and fertilizer. The Forest Department imposes penalty and the land is not allotted to us. We are paid Rs. 2 for cultivating the land in addition to some food three times a day.

10. *Bansra* (Bagidora Tehsil) : I am a barbar. I earn my livelihood by shaving others. The *sevak* indulges in untouchability. he absuses me. He has also beaten me. I have no house, no wife. I live with somebody in some way. I lodged a complaint against the *sevak*. The lawsuit is now going on. This was against the untouchability law. He also threatens me and prevents me from going to work. The cases have been going on for the last 12 months. The *sevak* does not want to come to a compromise. He threatens to kill me.

11. *Nathu Ram* (Bagidora Tehsil) : Everywhere there is bribery. The government is doing so much for us, but the government officials demand fees for everything. I have five to six acres of land. I have five sons, all of whom are married. None of

them has a *tapra* (hut), nor land. One boy works as a peon in a school. He has not got his salary for the past four months.

12. *Bidla* (Village Bansala, Tehsil Bagidora) : I was a *sagri*. Later the government gave me land. However, it was stony. The Collector told the *Patwari* to change the land. However, the *Patwari* has still not done it. The Sarpanch also gave an order, i.e. the land lying idle may be used for farming. There are 20 acres among 4 persons who have been recently freed from *sagri*. Now we must get this land.

13. *Raman* (Village Tanda, Tehsil Sajjangarh) : We are three brothers and have five acres of land among us. We all live in one *tipri* (hut). We do not have any bullock. We work for making bricks. We go from village to village with the contractor for making bricks. We have to eat on our own. He gives Rs. 12 for making 1,000 bricks. Four persons have to work the whole day for preparing 1,000 bricks. The wage, therefore, comes to Rs. 3 for one person for one day.

14. *Kalu* (Village Mandela, Tehsil Garhi) : Traditionally a grinder. I have been operating an indigenous grinding machine for *atta*. New machines have taken up this job even in villages, and, therefore, nobody wants my machine. One person earns and five persons eat in the family.

APPENDIX-II

SMALL GROUP WORK ON VILLAGE PROBLEMS

Specimens from Kotra Camp (Rajasthan) (February 3–8, 1979)

Sixty odd participants were divided among five groups on the basis of their Panchayat and village cluster. They sat together, discussed their perceptions about their problems and came to a consesus. One of them was named by them to report the conclusions of their discussions to the community. The following is a brief of the points raised by the various groups :

Group 1 : Report by a participant from village Badli and by Anil Kumar, former Dy. Sarpanch from Gopeepla.

1. Faced continuously with the problem of shortage of grain. Our crop does not come properly on time. We do not have any food, any work. Many a time we live on *poovar* (a type of grass) and sometimes also eat *chapati* made of grass.
2. We don't have any land. The Patwari harasses us all the time. he threatens, even beats people and gets their land vacated. For taking possession of surplus land bribe has to be paid to him.
3. No adult education facility. Education is lacking. There are two primary schools. One in village Badli with 30 children and another in village Gopeepla with 32 children up to class V.
4. No hospital. We cannot come to Kotra in rains. Have to go without any treatment most of the time.
5. No irrigation facility. There are 3 to 4 wells in Badli and 6 to 7 in a nearby village. But the level is higher than the river. Water does not come into the wells. Saber river is nearby, but no advantage.
6. Our village Gopeepla is surrounded by two rivers and there are no roads. We need a dam on the river in Umaria village. Without road we will not get electricity. We see all these facilities across the river in the Gujarat area. To our great misfortune we see the water from Vakal river flowing wastefully like blood from our body.
7. The Cooperative Credit Society in Badli is captured by one family. Secretary is the son, father is the Chairman and their *muneem* (accountant) the Treasurer. These shopkeepers have monopolized the Credit Society and give us loans on

high interest. They give Rs. 400 and take a receipt for Rs. 500. Sometimes they take a receipt for even Rs. 800 by paying only Rs. 400. The Sarpanch is trying to get the building of the Panchayat Bhavan constructed next door to his shop and residence. This will obviously benefit him in his business.

Hari Krishna, Sarpanch, reported that there was not even a Primary School in Bordi Khurd and Bordi Kalan.

Group 2 : (Sundrap, Kotra Chhavni, Kandi, Gandhi Sarana and Nayabas), Report by a participant from Kandi Village).

1. Grim problem of unemployment. Some people get work on road construction in exchange of 2 to 3 kilos of grain. Here also the Sarpanch deducts his share. The labourers thus employed are about 190 spread over four villages (Nayabas, Subri, Gandhi Sarana, Kotra Chhavni).
   There are no agricultural workers here. No scope for employing them on these small farms. People have to go out of their village to far-of places in search of work and have to be away for about eight months in a year. Many go to Himmat Nagar in Gujarat and other places and do odd jobs.
   We feel that there should be factories and small industrial type work as well as more facilities for agriculture in the area.
2. All kinds of illegal taxes, i.e. loot going on. The police treat the thieves and *Sahukar* (honest) in the same way, and take bribe from both. The police ask for *tampa* (bribe). This is a tax which they take for responding to a complaint and to take any work in their hands for the villagers. They do not work without such bribes and illegal taxes.
3. Public hospital is small. We want a big hospital with adequate medicines and doctors.
4. Continuous harassment by the shopkeepers. They weigh things in such a way that they take more when we give them and give less when we take. No accounts are kept. This is *loot vyapar* (dishonest trade). We take small loans from them and have to pay back two rupees for one rupee in two days. Failing this, the shopkeepers depute their *naukars* (servant musclemen) who are their pathans. The common saying here is that Naukar Bhai is coming. He will now beat us. In this way the village people are terrified and intimidated by the shopkeepers. There are instances where a villager (in village Kandi) took some chillies worth 25 paise.

He could not pay these paise within two days. The *naukars* then came and the villager was forced to work for one full day without any wage.

In village Gopeepla a villager took Rs. 40 from a shopkeeper. He could not pay back. His servant beat him up mercilessly and called him filthy names. In this quarrel, the shopkeeper also got slightly injured. A case was registered against the villager. He ran away from the village. Ultimately he was caught. He paid Rs. 20 to police, returned Rs. 40 plus Rs. 10 to the shopkeeper and in addition he was challaned. The case is still pending in the court. The villager will have to spend much more money by way of bribe or fees to the *vakeel* in order to get release from this case. Failing this he might be sentenced and put into jail.

The *soni* (goldsmith) is another source of harassment. He would not give any loan without some gold ornament or silver ornament mortgaged to him. He charges 10 paise as interest for one rupee per month. The time limit is usually from one to two years. Many a time he plays tricks and sees to it that the villager is unable to take the ornament back within the time limit. In this way he gets the ornament for just nothing.

There should be arrangement for *sarkari vyaj* (government interest), some kind of bank arrangement from where we can draw loans on reasonable interest.

Group 3 : (Representing Khaujuria, Mandva, Kookara, Jhad).

1. No work. Some of us are getting work for food but from where to get clothes and other necessities. No facilities for *pillai*, i.e. irrigation. Wells are without water. Not enough even for drinking.
2. No facilities for adult education.
3. No hospital. Doctors never come from Kotra. We have always to go to Kotra. It is difficult to go in rains. Many a time we have to physically carry sick persons on our shoulders across rivers and hills to go to Kotra. We do not get medical treatment.
4. No Post Office.
5. No work for the educated. There are some educated up to class XI.
6. Difficult to get forest work without bribes. No forest land for cattle. The forest people have put their *gote* (boundary) everywhere. Leaving no land for us.

7. There is no bus service. There are some private buses, who charge a lot of much money.

Group 4 : Report by Hari Krishnan, Sarpanch of village Mahidi.

1. *Problems concerning our homes and families :*

   (i) Our families are large, generally 5 to 7 children, and we have no land and no houses. The land is hilly and not fertile. It is not levelled, therefore, not good for agriculture.

   (ii) No facilities for fertilizer. Due to this, our crop is meagre. We do not get enough food. The crops are *jawar, kadru* (a kind of coarse grain), cotton, mustard. All these depend on rains. When there is more rain, all is washed out, when there is less rain everything dies. Generally, therefore, we have poor crop and not enough food.

2. *Problems of villages :*

   (i) No facility for irrigation. There are about a hundred wells in the Panchayat. While digging wells, we are faced with stones. There is only one Compressor Machine in the Panchayat Samiti; we send it here and there, with the result that no one properly uses it and most wells remain incomplete. There are only riany season wells with *kachcha pani*, i.e. no permanent use of water. Out of 100 wells, only 25 are in working condition with *kachcha* water and 75 are out of order. There are only 3 *pucca* wells in 3 villages. Others have to go there even for getting drinking water. Fifty per cent of the wells have been built on loans from the Small Farmers' Development Agency; 75 wells are incomplete even after the grants were given.

3. *Problems of the Panchayat :*

   (i) There is no Panchayat building. We are in a rented building. No road connecting Kotra with panchayats

> and other places. We are in between Gujarat (Himmat Nagar) and Rajasthan (Udaipur), the two district headquarters. We don't know where to go. In between these two we are treated as *lavaris* (orphans). Dividing four villages there is a small plot of land which belongs to Gujarat. This creates a lot of difficulties for us. We do not know where we belong. Many of us, therefore, feel that those neighbouring villages should go to Gujarat, so that our problems can be solved. We see a lot of development work going on there.

At the same time we have to come by crossing rivers and nullahs because there are no roads in the village. Even during sickness we have to go to Kotra with our sick people. Many times we could not go there.

No facilities for cattle and their treatment. We can go to Lambadia in Gujarat, 10 km. away, where we can get treatment, but it is also far off. There was a nurse at the sub-centre of the Primary Hearlth Centre in our area. Now that nurse has also been withdrawn and has been posted at the PSC Headquarters. Her salary is charged to the Panchayat budget. It is necessary that the nurse is posted back at our Panchayat and steps are taken to give us a hospital.

Some time ago a foundation stone was laid for a dam. This was done during 1974-75 by one of the then Rajasthan Ministers. Even a canal has been built. But unfortunately there is no dam. It is almost like building doors for a house even when there is no house. Not even a map of the house. They have put stones here and there but there is no boundary or dam anywhere. We hear that there are Rs. 29 lakhs for this dam. This was mentioned in November last year by Shri Boru Lal, MLA from Gogoonda. He also said that Rs. 1 lakh had been released for this purpose. However, no work has still been started.

Shopkeepers, mostly grain merchants, harass people very much. These persons enter one area with just one *potli* (small bag) and gradually spread their legs all around. They make money in all transactions. Give loans on our products and charge more from us when we purchase the same from them. For example, they would pay only Rs. 2 for one kilo of cotton, whereas the market price is Rs. 2.50. They would say either cotton is not good or that Rs. 2.50 is a wholesale price and not retail price. They have many other ways of cheating us. They may say cotton is *phindkar* (wet). They, therefore, deduct five kilos from one quintal of cotton and take away in this way several kilos of cotton. If we ask for proper price, they threaten not to take our goods.

Group 4 : (Villages Sikladairi, Mahdi and Mathara) Report by Mani Shankar.

1. Harassment by the shopkeepers and businessmen. The cloth which costs Rs. 9 per metre is sold by them at Rs. 10 per metre. They try all methods to get customers indebted to them.
2. No hospital in the area.
3. As there is no bridge on the river Saber and no roads available, no transport facilities are there. There was a proposal for building a bridge on the river Saber or on the Waav Naka and it is heard that a budget of Rs. 40 lakhs was sanctioned for this purpose. Nothing so far has come of it.
4. There are two wells with only *kachcha* water. As there is wheat crop near the wells, it is difficult for our cattle to drink water. They don't get water even during the rains. There is an urgent need for a tank in the area. There is a Sickla tank, but it is *khoda*, i.e. without water.
5. There is no Post Office.
6. Primary School is housed in a *kachcha* building which leaks throughout the rains. It is difficult to go to the school.
7. The forest people include even the revenue land in the forest area just to harass the villagers and to get some bribe.
8. In the Khajuria Panchayat, Kolia village has a population of 300, but there is no school. Many other villages like this are without a school.
9. The Cooperative Society asked for Rs. 600 back for a loan of Rs. 300 for two years. Some four years ago, one tribal sold a buffalo to a shopkeeper. After four years the buffalo got sick. The shopkeeper brought it back to the tribal saying that he had done some kind of magic on the cattle and that he should take it back and return his money. All pleas that the buffalo had been with the shopkeeper for four years and he had got all the milk and *ghee* from it proved of no avail. The policemen sided with the shopkeeper by taking a bribe and he put the tribal in jail.

APPENDIX-III

SELF-REPORTS OF SMALL GROUP WORK ON VILLAGE PROBLEMS

Specimens from Ambamata (Pratapgarh Camp) (June 3-7, 1979)

Group 1 : (Villages : Gopar Pura, Sawnli Putar, Lalpura, Panch Imli) Reporter : Suraj Mal, about 22 years, educated up to class X.

We scheduled tribe people (Meenas) do not get service (jobs). We go for interviews but are excluded by manipulation. We do not have land and so no farming. Some people have some land but there is no irrigation, no canal. There is no light (electricity) here. We do not get kerosene oil. The forest ranger harasses us and prevents us from taking wood. He wants bribe. We have made an application for loan for house building. We have to go from place to place and person to person. Still no loan has been given. The contractor gives only Rs. 3 when we work on tank construction, whereas the minimum wage is Rs. 5. We do not get any justice from the Courts. They go on giving us different dates and then call us in the rainy season. It is the difficult for us to go. They harass us in order to get some money. When we are attacked and/or are caught in a fight or quarrel we go to the police station to report, then they ask for money. Even after giving Rs. 400-500 they do not do our work. I took land from a Harijan at mortgage of Rs. 2,000. The land belongs to a *bhangee* (Harijan). Now we cannot do any farming on the land; he is not giving back the money.

There is no school in Lalpura. The nearest is about 2 km way.

There is no arrangement for adult education.

Kanhaya Lal taught for about 2 years in adult education classes in Panch Imli. He was not paid any money. We do not know who has taken away this money.

Group 2 : (Villages : Pandva, Gamada Dolle, Damakundi, Jolar, Mungri) Reporter : Ram Chander, about 28 years – Sarpanch.

The Patwari wants a bribe for everything. The police do not do anything for us without money. We are illiterate and, therefore, we pay Rs. 400-500 even for every simple matters. We have to arrange for this money by selling our cattle or putting land on mortgage. The Forest Department does not help us at all. There is a rule that we can take some wood from the forest for building our houses. This is allowed free. The Ranger comes in the way. There is no end to the loans we take from mahajans. We took some loan from the Panchayat Samiti. Somebody came and took this money from us. Did not give any receipt. We trusted him. He is now not seen anywhere. We have to still return the loan to the Panchayat Samiti.

There is no school in Damakundli. The nearest is in Pulia 4 km. away. Population of the village is 250. We have many social evils like *dapa* (bride-price). This *dapa* is given by the boy's family and they take a loan for this purpose.

We have formed an Adivasi Samiti to fight against social evils. We have some 200 members in the Pandva Tehsil. This has been registered at Jaipur.

There is no arrangement for adult education. We have tried and going for village to village have prepared a list of people who would like to attend adult education classes. We had sent this list to a person who came here; in this connection nothing has happened thereafter.

We ourselves can run these classes and we can do this easily in Rajpurai and Dam Dumri.

We have land but it is not of much use because of lack of irrigation. There is a tank in Jalar village, but the water does not stay. Wells also need to be deepened. There is a river Sangla in the area and it is possible to put a dam there. We have been corresponding for this purpose. It is necessary to keep godowns for fertilizer in villages. We have to go 6 to 8 miles for getting fertilizer. The Primary Agriculture Cooperative Society is there, but some have become members wrongfully. Some is there, but some have become members wrongfully. Some of use want to become members but we are not given the chance. Some Panchayat members are also elected wrongfully.

We do not have any post office and no facility for a nurse or compounder. During the rains, there is water everywhere and we cannot go anywhere.

Group 3 : Report by Shanti Lal, 22 years.

There is a middle school in the village but no building. No seating arrangement for children during the rains. They are, therefore, given holidays. All 150 children and 8 teachers sit in one room. There are only two rooms. One is adjoining a nullah which is flooded during the rains and children cannot cross it, preventing them from going to school. There is an urgent need for a bridge over this nullah. In Ambamata there is a well in the Khera area. This can irrigate some 300 acres of land. We collected Rs. 6,000 – 7,000 and have already installed there a motor. Connections have also been made. Unfortunately, there is no water in the well which requires digging and deepening. This was to be done by the government, as per the understanding, as their contribution. They have done nothing to implement this project. The result is that the motor has been lying idle and may be spoiled. The government officials say that there is no need for deepening the well, as the purpose would be served by collecting water at the nullah. This has never happened and collecting water is a difficult task. The BDO has also been transferred since then.

There is a Primary Health Centre, but there is no building for it. It is housed in a rented building. The landlord wants this to be vacated. Some time back we came to this place (the venue of the training programme at Ambamata – the *Dharmshala*) and wanted to occupy it for the Health Centre. The temple priest objected and prevented us from doing so. We also broke cpen the room but did not occupy because there would have been a quarrel.

We don't have any Cooperative here for fertilizer. I myself wanted to become a member of such a society and the Panchayat wanted Rs. 20 as membership fee. I was not taken as a member in another village and now my village also does not take me as member. The Manager does not agree and the Panchayat wants a bribe. The Panchayat gave us some government land and we have been using it for the past five years. The Sarpanch has taken a bribe from us but he has not yet given possession of the land to us.

A boy stood up and reported : Under the Antyodaya they gave 10 milk goats and one he-goat. The doctor took Rs. 100 as bribe for passing these cattle. The cost of these cattle was estimated at Rs. 2,000 for which a receipt was taken. In fact, the cattle cost only Rs. 1,500. The rest has been taken as bribe including the fee for the doctor. Thus,our loan is far Rs. 2,000 which we have to pay back in instalments of Rs. 300 each.

One year ago another person (Sukhlal) from Batmeshvar village got a card under the Antyodaya scheme. He was to have been given a loan of Rs. 2,000 for opening a small *bidi* shop. This loan has not still been given.

Group 4 : (Villages : Birawali, Arned, Gomteshwar, Clipat) Reporter : Kanhyalal, 20 years, educated up to class XI.

We don't have any adult education classes. No village in this area has such a class. Two days ago we held a meeting and some 50 to 60 people came showing their desire to attend adult education classes. We have also a teacher (Phool Chand). He is educated up to class VIII. We propose to start classes on our own.

For our cattle there is no drinking water. The wells get dry very soon. We have to bring water from a distance of about a mile. We have land with black soil and we get one crop during the rains. We get cotton crop. This is not enough because there is no irrigation. People in Antyodaya go for construction work. They get Rs. 5 per day on road construction. Now workers get only Rs. 5. We have built a school under the Food for Work Programme.

Group 5 : (Villages : Panmori, Amblikhera, Dorr, Goria) Reporter : Amrit Ram, 20 years old, educated up to class VII.

There is great difficulty of drinking water. There are some wells, but no water. There is a tank and it is possible to instal a motor. For this the villagers of Panmori collected Rs. 10,000 but the government did nothing. The money had, therefore, to be refunded to the villagers. Some time ago there was a fire in the village and there was no way to contact officials. There is a need for at least one telephone in the village. There are no roads also.

Nobody can get admitted to Pratapgarh Hospital without giving a bribe. I myself went for 10 days. I also took the Sarpanch. Then also the doctor took Rs. 20 and gave me a prescription. I was then admitted. There is a demand of bribe everywhere. (He told this with great anger.)

The *patidars* have taken all the land. There is no land even for building houses for us. The *patidars* have snatched away lands of the tribals. This is totally illegal and many times there have been fights. In one case we collected Rs. 40 by contribution and gave to Shri Sharma to get a medical certificate. Now the case is going on in Court. The Patwari has taken land from *chamars* and kept this with Barani. They go to farms with guns. In Gamaria village people have paid Rs. 100 to Rs. 200 as bribe to the Patwari. Half the people do not have any land. We have gone to the BDO and have also met the Patwari. Land has been taken back from people after remaining in their possession for three years. We also met the MLA, but he did not do anything.

In Rathagana village, people gave receipts with their thumb impressions to some official without getting money from the Cooperative Society. The official obtained all this money from the Society and then disappeared. In another instance someone took away the share of a loan which the Cooperative gave for house-building by giving false receipts to the Society. This has been going on for the past four years. In yet another case, everyone deposited Rs. 150 with the Secretary of the Cooperative Society (they named the person). Some 45 persons gave this money. He told us that he would get us Rs. 4,000 each for building a house. Thereafter, he just ran away with the money. We reported the matter to the Panchayat Samiti, but nothing has happened so far.

There is a Vakil Sarpanch (they named him also) but he does not take any interest. He hardly comes to the village. I am myself Sarpanch, but what can I do alone. People are afraid.

In Rathagana village, Bhagirath took a loan of Rs. 60. He gave back Rs. 50 and after 2 years paid back Rs. 10 by way of interest. Now the mahajan wants Rs. 300. He himself is a *meghwal*. The villager had worked for the Mahajan for 2 years. After all this the Mahajan insists on taking Rs. 10 per month from him. All his prayers have failed.

BIBLIOGRAPHY

Ahmed, B. (1971) : "Political Stratification of the Indian Electorate", *EPW*, Annual Number, 6(3-5), 251-258.

Almond A.G. and Sidney Verba, (1963) : *The Civic Culture : Political Attitudes and Democracy in Five Nations*, Princeton, N.J. : Princeton University Press.

Anand, Sudhir and Amartya Sen (1992) : "Human Development Index : Methodology and Measurement", *Background Paper for Human Development Report 1993*, UNDP, New Delhi : Oxford University Press.

Arora, S.K. (1969) : "Exploring Political Predisposition, Efficacy and Cynicism in Rural Andhra Pradesh", *Behavioural Sciences and Community Development*, 3(2), 126-138.

Ashraf, M. Siddique (1975) : "Socio-Political Consciousness among Industrial Workers : An Area Study", *Indian Journal of Industrial Relations*, 11(1), 41-51.

Atal, Yogesh (1969) : "Citizens Sense of Political Efficacy", *EPW*, Annual Number, January, 171-178.

Bandyopadhyay, D. (1986) : "Land Reforms in India : An Analysis" *EPW*, XXI, A50-A56.

Bailey, F.G. (1973) : The Peasant View of Bad Life in Shanin, Teodar (Ed.) *Peasants and Peasant Societies*, Penguin Education Series, 299-321.

Bloom, S.B.; Davis, Allison and Hers Robert (1965) : *Compulsory Education for Cultural Deprivation*, New York : Holt, Rinerhart and Winston.

Blumberg, P. (1968) : *Industrial Democracy : The Sociology of Participation*, London : Constable.

Brinkerhoff, Berick W. (1979) : "Inside Public Bureaucracy : Empowering Managers to Empower Clients" *Rural Development Participation Review*, 1(1), 7-9.

Chandra, Navin and Prayag Mehta (1984) : *People's Self Action for Development*, New Delhi : National Labour Institute.

Census (1971), Registrar General of Census, New Delhi : GOI.

——, (1981) : Registrar General of Census, New Delhi : GOI.

Chikermane, D.V. (1968) : "The State Reports on Wastage and Stagnation : A Study of Wastage in Primary Education", *Education Quarterly*, 20(3), 1-13.

Das, A.N. (1976) : "In Bonded Freedom", *EPW*, 11, 724-726.

Deutach, Martin *et al* (eds) (1968) : *Social Class, Race and Psychological Development*, New York : Holt, Rinehart, and Winston.

Dreze, Jean and Sen, Amartya (1989) : *Hunger and Public Action*, Exford : Clarendon Press.

Economic Times (1991) : "The Economy/Employment : The Growing Concern", Sept. 30, New Delhi.

Elias, N. and J.L. Scotson (1965) : *The Established and the Outsiders*, London : Frank Cass.

Economic and Social Commission for Asia and Pacific (1982) : *Poverty, Productivity and Participation : An Analysis of Some Recent Asian Experience*, Bangkok : United Nations.

FAO (1980) : *Review and Analysis of Agrarian Reform and Rural Development in Developing Countries since the Mid-1960s*, World Conference on Agrarian Reform and Rural Development-INF-3, Rome.

Freire Paulo (1974) : *Education for Critical Consciousness*, London : Sheed and Ward.

Gopalan, C. (1983) : "Deprivation and Development", *Economic and Political Weekly*, XVIII, 2163-68.

Huizer, Gerrit (1972) : *Revolutionary Potential of Peasants in America*, Mass : Lexington.

——, (1973) : Community Development, Land Reform and Political Participation in Teodar Shanin (Ed.) *Peasants and Peasant Societies*, Penguin Education in Modern Sociology Readings, 389-411.

Hunt, J. McVicker (1968) : "Environment, Development and Scholostic Achievement" in Deutach, Martin *et al* (eds.) *Social Class, Rase and Psychological Development*.

——, (1973) : *The Challenges of Incompetence and Poverty : Papers on the Role of Early Education*, Urbana : University of Illinois Press.

Inkeles, A. and Smith, A.H. (1974) *Becoming Modern*, Cambridge, MA : Harward University Press.

International Labour Organisation (1975) : *ILO Convention 141 : Organisations of Rural Workers and their Role in Economic and Social Development*, Geneva : ILO.

——, (1977) : *Poverty and Landlessness in Rural Asia*, Geneva : ILO.

——, (1982) : Convention No. 141 in *International Labour Convention and Recommendations*, 1919-1981, Geneva : ILO, 15-24.

——, (1982a) : Recommendation No. 127, in *International Labour Convention and Recommendations*, Geneva, ILO, 151-157.

——, (1984) : "Speech of WHO Director General" quoted in *International Centre for Advanced Technical and Vocational Training Bulletin*, 40, February.

——, (1986) : *The Participation of the Rural Poor in Development*, Geneva.

Iyer, K.G. and Das, A.N. (1976) : "Orissa : A Study of Poverty and Bondage", *National Labour Institute Bulletin*, 5, 178-84.

Jayaraman, M. (1967) : *Stagnation and Wastage in Primary Schools*, New Delhi : NCERT.

Jensen, Arthur R. (1968) : "Social Class and Verbal Learning" in Deutsch, Martin *et al* (eds.) *Social Class, Race and Psychological Development*.

Korten, David, C. and Norman T. Uphoff (1981) : "Bureaucratic Reorientation for Participatory Rural Development", Washington DC : National Association of School of Public Affairs and Administration, *Working Paper No. 1*.

Kothari, Rajni (1967) : "Political Change of 1967", *EPW* 6(3, 4&5), 229-250.

Maharaj, R.N.; and Iyer, K.G. (1975) : "Field Report from Rajgir (Nalanda, Bihar) Part I : The Rural Poor and Their Problem" *National Labour Institute Bulletin*, 5, 189-97.

——, (1976) : "A Change Strategy for Rural India", *NLI Bulletin*, 5, 189-197.

Mehta, Prayag (1969) : *Achievement, Motive in High School Boys and Training for it*, New Delhi : National Council of Education Research and Training.

Mehta, Prayag; Pareek H. and Sharma D. (1972) : "From Impotent Anger to Potent Self : A Leadership Laboratory", *Indian Management*, 1-9.

Mehta, Prayag (1975) : *Efficacy, Participation and Politics*, New Delhi : PADC, Unpublished Manuscript.

——, (1975a) : *Election Campaign : Anatomy of Mass Influence*, New Delhi : National.

——, (1976) : *Managing Motivation in Education*, Ahmedabad : Sahitya Mudranalaya.

——, (1976a) : From Economism to Democratic Commitment : The Role of Workers' Participation, *Vikalpa*, 1(4), 3946.

——, (1976b) : Analysing Imagery for Social Efficacy, New Delhi : National Labour Institute, *Mimeo*.

Mehta, Prayag (1976c) : "Work Satisfaction and Democratic Outlook", *NLI Bulletin*, 2(6), 231-234.

——, (1976d) : "Alienated Middle Manager", *National Labour Bulletin*, NLI, 2, 94-96.

——, (1977) "Changing Higher Education through Student Participation in Decision-making", *Institution Building at Education and Research*, ed. by Ravi Mathai *et al*, Delhi : All India Management Association, 54-59.

——, (1977a) : "Employee Motivation and Work Satisfaction in a Public Enterprise", *Vikalpa*, 2(3), 223-236.

——, (1978) : "Subjective and Objective Factors in Employees Satisfaction in Life and Work", *Indian Journal of Industrial Relations*, 2(13) : 433-444.

——, (1978a) : "Workers Rising Aspirations and Work Organisation", *Yojana*, May.

——, (1979) : "Exposure to Mass Media and Leisure Time Behaviour of Youth" *Indian Journal of Youth Affairs*, 1(3), 9-21.

——, (1981) : Political Processes and Behaviour. In ICSSR *Survey of Research in Psychology*, 1971-1976 (Part 2) New Delhi : Popular Prakashan.

——, (1982) : *Manual for Personal Achievement, Social Achievement and Influence Motivation*, New Delhi : NLI.

——, (1983) : "Political Efficacy and Participation in Socio-Economic Eevelopment", *Journal of Rural Development*, 2(6), 563-570.

——, (1983a) : "Mortgaged Child Labour and Women Beedi Workers of Vellore", *Mainstream*, September, 15-17.

——, (1985) : *Quality of Working Life and Work Democratisation : Some Strategies and Methodologies*, Delhi : Faculty of Management Studies, University of Delhi.

——, (1985a) : "Participative Management of Rural Development." *The Administrator*, 30(1), 73-90.

——, (1988) : "Organising for Empowering the Poor" in Pradip Khandwalla (ed) *Social Development : A New Role for the Organisational Science*, New Delhi : Sage, 174-185.

——, (1989) : *Bureaucracy, Organisational Behaviour and Development*, New Delhi : Sage.

——, (1989a) : *Participation and Organisation Development*, Jaipur : Rawat.

——, (1990) : *Integrate Adult Education with Life : Feedback from Rajasthan*, New Delhi : PADC.

Mehta, Prayag (1991) : *Energizing Agriculture Extension : Involvement of Voluntary Agencies*, New Delhi : PADC.

——, (1992) : *Movement for Total Literacy : The Case of Sonebhadra*, New Delhi : PADC.

——, (1993) : "Collective Action for Social Entitlement", *Asian Seminar on Social Security Programme in Developing Countries*, New Delhi : Social Security Association of India.

——, (1994) : *Social Achievement Motivation : Values, Needs and Work Organisation*, New Delhi : Concept.

——, (1994a) : "Empowering People for Social Achievement : Motivation for Sustainable Development" in Ravindra N. Kanungo and Manuel Mendonca (Eds.) *Work Motivation : Models for Developing Countries*, New Delhi : Sage.

Minhas, B.S. (1991) : "Education Deprivation and Its Role : A Spoiler of Access to Better life in India" *Technical Report No. 9104*, New Delhi : Indian Statistical Institute.

Ministry of Education (1966) : *Education and National Development*, Education Commission, 1964-66, Ministry of Education, New Delhi : Govt. of India, 139-143.

——, (1973) : *Farmers' Training and Functional Literacy : A Pilot Evaluation Study in Lucknow District*, New Delhi : DAE.

——, (1975) : *Achievement, Constraints and Lessons*, New Delhi : DAE.

——, (1976) : *Education in India*, New Delhi : Govt. of India.

Ministry of Finance (1975) : *India : Pocket Book of Economic Information 1973-74*, New Delhi : Deptt. of Economic Affairs.

Ministry of Health and Family Planning (1981) : *Report of the Working Group on Health for All by 2000 AD*, New Delhi : Govt. of India.

——, (1985) : *Challenge of Education*, New Delhi : Govt. of India.

Ministry of HRD, Department of Education (1986) *National Policy on Education*, New Delhi : GOI.

——, (1988) : *National Literacy Mission*, New Delhi : GOI.

——, (1990) : *Towards an Englightened and Human Society*, Committee for Review of National Policy on Education, New Delhi : GOI.

——, (1990a) : *Annual Report of the Ministry of HRD, 1989-90*, New Delhi : GOI.

——, (1990b) : *Education for All by 2000*, New Delhi : GOI.

——, (1991) : *Guide Book for Mass Campaign for Total Literacy*, New Delhi : GOI.

Ministry of Labour (1972) : *Handbook of Training Facilities in Bihar*, Govt. of India : CIRTES.

——, (1972a) : *Handbook of Training Facilities in Orissa*, Govt. of India : CIRTES.

——, (1980) : *Standard Note* by Director General of Labour Welfare, New Delhi : GOI.

Ministry of Home Affairs (1978) : *Report of the Working Group on Tribal Development during Mid-Term Plan 1978-83*, Govt. of India.

Ministry of Rural Reconstruction (1979) : *Report of the Study Team on Rural Employment*, Govt. of India : 42-49.

——, (1979a) : *Guidelines on Rural Industries Component of IRDP and Trysem*, Govt. of India : 8-9.

Mishra, Grish K. (1987) : "Development Programmes for the Urban Poor : Some Issues" presented at the National Seminar on Development Programmes for the Urban Poor, New Delhi : IIPA, February.

Mukherjee, Nirmal (1985) : "Democracy and Development", *Future*, December, 6-13.

Mussen, P. and Wyszynski, A. (1952) : Personality and Political Participation, *Human Relations*, 5, 65-82.

Naik, J.P. (1975) : *Policy and Performance in Indian Education, 1947-74*, Delhi : Orient Longman.

——, (1975a) : *Equality, Quality and Quantity : An Elusive Triangle in Indian Education*, Bombay : Allied Publishers.

Nandi, Ashish (1975) : "Acceptance and Rejection of Democratic Norms in India", *Indian Journal of Psychology*, 50 : 265-78.

National Labour Institute (1984) : "Agrarian Relations and Rural Workers Organisations", *NLI Bulletin*, 10(4), Full Issue.

NCERT (1976) : *A Pilot Project on Non-Formal Education, Bhumiadhar*, Nainital, U.P. New Delhi : Deptt. of School Education.

Pai, K.K. (1976) : "Accelerating Development Process among Small and Marginal Farmers : A Conceptual Model and Practical Significance", Paper presented in a *National Seminar on new Agricultural Technology and Extension Strategy for Small and Marginal Farmers*, Punjab Agri. University.

Pareek, Udai (1986) : "Dynamics of Decentralisation", *B. Mehta Memorial Lecture*, Jaipur.

Passi, B.G. (1974) : Educational Evaluation and Examinations : A Trend report in M.B. Buch (ed) *A Survey of Research in Education*, Baroda : CABE, Baroda University.

Pateman, Carole (1970) : *Participation and Democratic Theory*, Cambridge University Press.

Piaget, J. (1952) : *The Origin of Intelligence in Children*, New York : International University Press.

Planning Commission (1978) : *Sixth Five Year Plan : Draft Outline*, Govt. of India.

——. (1980) : *Sixth Five Year Plan*, 1980-85, Govt. of Inida.

——. (1992) : *JRY—A Quick Case Study*, 1991-92, Government of India.

Rahman, Anisur (1983) : *Sarilakas : A Pilot Project for Stimulating Grass-Roots Participation in the Philippines*, Geneva : ILO.

Raj Krishna (1978) : "Nehru-Gandhi Polarity and Economic Policy", *Mainstream*, August 5 : 8-12 & 34.

Rath, R. (1974) : Teaching-Learning Problems of the Disadvantaged Tribal Children. *The Indian Academy of Applied Psychology, 12th Annual Conference*, Utkal Univerty : Bhubaneswar.

Reserve Bank of India (1972) : *All India Debt and Investment Survey 1971-72—Assets and Liabilities of Rural Households as on 30 June 1971*, Statistical Table, Uttar Pradesh.

Ross, Aileen D. (1969) : *Student Unrest in India : A Comparative Approach*, Montreal : McGill Queen's University Press.

Roy, Ramashray (1975) : "Citizen Orientations and Patterns of Political Instability" in D.L. Seth (Ed.) *Citizen and Partieis—Aspects of Competitive Politics in India*, New Delhi : Allied Publishers.

Saran, K. (1976) : "Law and Bonded Labour System", *National Labour Institute Bulletin*, 11, 31-34.

Selbourne, David (1977) : *An Eye to India : The Unmasking of a Tyranny*, Penguin Books.

University Grants Commission (1971) : *Information Paper*, May 9 : 17-29.

——, (1971a) : *Report of the Committee on Governance of Universities and Colleges*, New Delhi : 72.

Szal, R.J. (1979) : "Popular Participation, Employment and the Fulfilment of Basic Needs", *International Labour Review*, 118(1).

United Nations Development Programme (1990) : *Human Development Report 1990*, New York : Oxford University Press.

——, (1993) : *Human Development Report, 1993*, New Delhi : Oxford University Press.

UNESCO (1975) : "Results, Achievements, Progress" in *Achievement, Constrains and Lesson*, Ministry of Education, New Delhi : Govt. of India.

INDEX